of computing specialists. From impartial advice on system design to installation and maintenance, we are here to help you get on with your business. No matter how large or small your system, Compaq treats every mission as critical. Call us today on 0845 270 4075.

(please quote 99CMM 12)

The Daily Telegraph

How to Set Up and Run Your Own Business

**FIFTHTEENTH
EDITION**

Helen Kogan

**KOGAN
PAGE**

First published in 1983

Thirteenth edition 1997
Fourteenth edition 1998
Fifteenth edition 1999

Published by Kogan Page Limited for The Telegraph plc,
1 Canada Square, Canary Wharf, London E14 5DT

Kogan Page Limited
120 Pentonville Road
London N1 9JN

British Library Cataloguing in Publication Data
A CIP record for this book is available from the British Library.
ISBN 0 7494 3007 9

Typeset by Saxon Graphics Ltd, Derby
Printed and bound in Great Britain by Thanet Press Ltd, Margate

Contents

A small concern?

Don't worry. There are no charges on our business bank account.

Here's one less thing to worry about. If you're a sole trader or two person partnership, we offer a business bank account free of transaction charges until 31st December 2000.*

After that, if you run the account within certain defined transaction limits, you can still bank for free.

In addition our business bank account pays interest on credit balances and can be operated by phone, post or cash machine 24 hours a day.

For more information or to apply, simply call us, Monday to Friday 8am to 6pm quoting reference BBA00.

0800 056 5151

Business Bank Account  **ABBEY NATIONAL®**

Because life's complicated enough.

S47

Keeping the customer happy 61; Needs and
benefits 62; Advertising 63; Public relations 65;
Direct mail 66; The Internet 68; Shows and
exhibitions 69; Sales 70; Motivating salespeople 74;
Checklist 74

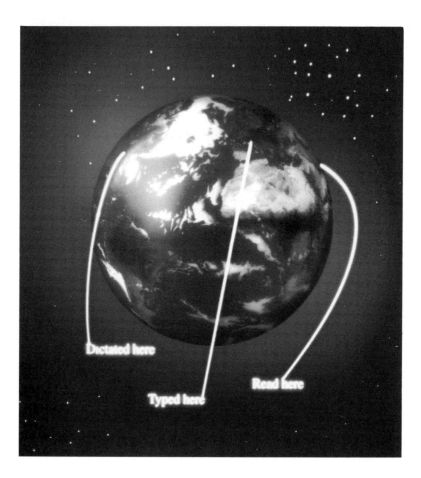

Dictated here

Typed here

Read here

Olympus has just shrunk the planet.

It is all down to a remarkable new dictation system called the D1000, a pocket recorder that makes Concorde look positively pedestrian as it whisks your words of wisdom halfway around the globe in less time than it takes to say "warp factor".

Such speed is down to a digital recording system that stores speech on a tiny memory card. The digitized sound can be played back like a normal tape with the added benefit of instant deletions, additions or editing in any part of the text.

Down load the files to your PC and things really start to take off. Attached to an e-mail, the highly compressed sound file can be zapped to wherever you choose, anywhere in the world, at the touch of a button.

If your words on the move form the basis of a formal report for example, the e-mail arrives at your PA's PC back at HQ.

And while you settle down to sleep on one side of the Atlantic, she is up with the lark, transcribing your dulcet tones with the help of a PC compatible headset and footswitch.

The moment you have finished whispering in her ear, the report is on the move again and at it's final destination long before you leave the land of dreams.

If all this sounds too good to be true, it is only fair to point out that there are alternatives. You could match such speed by blasting into orbit at the cost of a few billion. You could charter something supersonic to be at your beck and call for several tens of thousands.

Or you could keep your feet on the ground and splash out just £250 on the D1000.

Add one to your briefcase and we confidently predict that you will be over the moon.

Please telephone 0800 072 0070 for stockist information.

OLYMPUS D1000
DIGITAL VOICE RECORDER

Safe companies have healthier profits

A survey for the British Safety Council has identified a group of small private companies as lethal weapons in their handling of health and safety at work.

"These are businesses that have very low regard for staff safety or the law, yet believe they know it all," said Sir Neville Purvis, Director General of the Safety Council. "They have no professional support. Although they might take some (free) advice from the Chamber of Commerce, they won't budget for safety training and have learned nothing from previous accidents."

The British Safety Council provides a range of services to educate all organisations, regardless of size, on the importance of best practice for successful businesses in increasing productivity and profitability and helping to win new contracts and repeat business.

THE CONTRIBUTORS

The publishers would like to express their appreciation of the help given by the following contributors in the preparation of earlier editions of this book: Hugh Aldous, John Anisworth, Henry Ballantyne, Carol Barrie, John Blundell, Norman Boakes, Michael J Brookes, Geoffrey Burcher, David Byrne, Roy Chapman, The Charterhouse Group, Colin Davis, Henry Deschampsneufs, Robert Fleeman, Andrew Hamilton, Charles Hodder, Keith Jones, Jim Kerevan, Michael Killingley, Richard Lee, David Marcelline, Bill Packer, David Philip, Max Pullen, Michael Reader, Frank Rounthwaite, Pradesh Shah, Tony Timberlake, Michael Tomlinson, Frank Walker, Rodney Westhead, Ken White, David Wise, H H Yates and David Young.

The publishers are indebted to:

Roger Bennett

Heather Coath

Department of Trade and Industry

Brian Finch

Michael Malone

Graham Mott

Dave Patten

Royal Institute of Chartered Surveyors

for their help with updating the fifteenth edition of this book.

NOTE

Masculine pronouns have been used throughout this book. This stems from a desire to avoid ugly and cumbersome language, and no discrimination, prejudice or bias is intended.

Prime Health, Our Product Range

Prime Health, a wholly owned subsidiary of the Standard Life Group. Europe's largest mutual life assurance company, has become one of the UK's fastest growing health insurers since its launch in 1988. It offers a wide range of individual and company plans to over 350,000 customers and is currently fourth in the private medical insurance market.

The company attributes its success to product innovation, value for money and total commitment to its customers. Evidence of this commitment is demonstrated by Prime Health's achievement of ISO 9002 for customer care, its membership of the Insurance Ombudsman Bureau and its ongoing campaign to demystify the whole subject of private healthcare.

Prime Health has pioneered simplicity in PMI and recently repositioned its individual Primecare range to make choosing a policy easy. The range is built around the 'core' comprehensive Primecare plan, which provides cover in full for all eligible in-patient treatment, day care surgery, out-patient consultations and tests. In addition it provides valuable extra benefits such as home nursing, alternative medicine, psychiatric treatment and parent accomodation.

This is the basic model, but other plans in the range build on extra features such as holiday and business travel insurance, major dental expenses etc. or, if you're looking for lower cost premiums, offer a smaller core of benefits. The lower cost plans feature a unique customer declaration designed to ensure that people understand what they are purchasing.

As part of our ongoing commitment to making private healthcare easier to understand, Prime Health ensures that all literature is written in plain English and is easy to understand. As a consequence of this, we have been awarded the Clear English Standard from the Plain English Commission.

For more information on Prime Health's range of plans call

0800 77 99 55

Get a better deal on private healthcare

from 50p a day

Come to Prime Health to discover health insurance with a difference. With a full range of plans to meet every need, you can be certain we'll have exactly the cover to suit you.

And because we're part of Standard Life, Europe's largest mutual life assurance company, you can be confident Prime Health set out to deliver the best value health insurance available.

Just compare the cost of Prime Health's leading plan, Primecare, with those of other insurers:

Monthly premium for a single person, aged 35

Primecare	**£35.54**
BUPACare	£43.48
PPP Extensive	£53.91
Norwich Union Express Care	£55.80

Call
0800 77 99 55
to find out more

Quoting ref:
M17103NG

Prime Health
A member of the Standard Life Group

we'll help you get
your franchise off the ground

If you're looking at franchising, you need a bank with experience and understanding. We can offer you a wide range of financial services and all the support you require when you're starting your business. Find out more by sending for our free brochure using the coupon, or phone us on 0117 943 3089 and quote reference DT1. We'll be waiting to help your business take off.

Send this coupon to Lloyds TSB, Dept CB, FREEPOST, PO Box 112, Canons Way, Bristol BS1 5BR. Please send me information on Lloyds TSB Franchising Services.

Name _____

Telephone _____

Address _____

_____

Postcode _____

DT1

Published by Lloyds Bank Plc and TSB Bank plc, both of whose registered offices are at 71 Lombard Street, London EC3P 3BS.

Lloyds TSB
Business

1 | What Kind of Business?

This book is a basic introduction to the world of the self-employed and the small businessman. It has been written on the assumption that you have spent your working life to date as an employee, and that your knowledge of value added tax (VAT), National Insurance (NI), controlling a business and such matters is limited.

There are over three million people in business on their own today. Two and a quarter million are self-employed, and the remainder are directors of their own limited companies. Large numbers of people every month are setting up in business. Some 96 per cent of all firms are small businesses, accounting for 20 per cent of our gross national product. With big business laying people off, and cuts in local and central government, what is left for you to do? Either work for a small business or start up on your own.

So what do these small business people do? By far the most popular is the retail sector, followed by the building industry, two areas which are not performing well at present. Wherever there is a gap in the market, you are likely to find self-employed people trying to satisfy the demand for goods and services. From the shopkeeper, the builder and the farmer to the self-employed tobacco-taster and the self-employed golf course designer – you name it, the self-employed are doing it.

HAVE YOU A VIABLE PROPOSITION?

Two essential elements in a viable business proposition are the product (or service) and the people involved. Until the marketability of the product has been established, there is little point in proceeding further, but given a commercial product and a good management team, it will then be necessary to look carefully at the premises, equipment and financial resources necessary to start the business.

It is tempting to think that a novel idea has better prospects than a proven product; in practice it is not as simple as that.

If you plan to sell your product or service to an established market, are you sure that your sales projections are realistic for a business starting from scratch? You need to consider the size of the total market, whether it is expanding or contracting, the number of competitors active in it already and how the market is divided among them. Ask yourself what proportion of the market the new enterprise aims to capture in the first year, the second year and so on, and why people should buy from you instead of from someone else. How sensitive are your projections to the impact of a fairly small variation in market share achievements?

Finally, in reviewing your product, make sure that you have the legal right to produce and sell it. Legal advice may be necessary in order to safeguard the future of your project.

WHAT KIND OF BUSINESS?

Let us begin by looking at the initial stages of starting a business. If you are setting up as a sole trader, say a freelance consultant, with a turnover below the VAT threshold, no premises and no staff, and you are trading under your own name, then virtually all you have to do is tell the Inland Revenue and the Department of Social Security (DSS) of your change in status, and then begin to trade. However, once you reach the VAT threshold, use separate business premises, take on staff and trade perhaps as a limited company, the picture is very different.

The sole trader

The first question you need to ask yourself is, what form will my business take? The simplest way of going into business is to trade on your own and under your own name. The main point to bear in mind is that you are personally liable for all debts since you have no limited liability.

However, you may feel that your name is not the most striking, or the most easily remembered, so you may decide to trade under a name other than your own. In this case, as the name is not your own and therefore ownership of the business is not immediately apparent, it is necessary to show in three places your name and an address within Great Britain at which the service of documents will be effective. This must appear on all letters, orders, invoices, receipts and written demands for payments, and must be prominently displayed at all places in which the business is conducted, and to which customers and suppliers have access. You have what is known as a general statutory duty to divulge ownership of the business and an effective address within Great Britain at which a document may be served upon you. This you may have to do on demand, in writing. Even though you are trading under a name which is not your own, you are still personally liable for all debts.

Going into partnership

The same basic rules apply to a partnership as to the sole trader, the main difference being that you are working with someone else and not by yourself. It is also worth remembering that should your partner amass business debts, unknown to you, then in all likelihood you will be responsible for those debts (other than debts relating to purely personal matters) if your partner disappears.

You are strongly advised to have a partnership agreement drawn up by a solicitor in order to prevent difficulties arising from any future break-up of the partnership. This agreement needs to cover the basis on which the partners intend to work together, and should among other stipulations include:

☐ the procedures to be followed should one of the partners die or leave the business for any other reason;

☐   definition of the partners' remuneration;
☐   whether decisions are made jointly or separately.

If you are going into a partnership or starting up as a sole trader, remember that the statutory benefits to the self-employed, sickness benefit, for example, are considerably less than those for the employed. Permanent Health Insurance (PHI) policies, pensions, etc. all need to be considered. Ask your insurance broker to submit a number of quotes from different insurance companies.

The limited company

The main difference between trading as a company and trading as a partnership is the limited liability factor. The directors of a company are not personally liable for debts incurred by the company except for non-payment of NI contributions. Everyone's circumstances are different and there are different schools of thought; if you are thinking of going into business and of forming a limited company, get advice from an accountant or solicitor first. Do not rush into it without thought and good reasons.

There are four main matters to be dealt with in forming a company (in some instances your solicitor will be able to help):

☐   choosing a name;
☐   defining the business purpose of the company (its 'objects');
☐   settling its contribution and procedural rules (the company's 'Memorandum and Articles of Association');
☐   filing particulars with the Registrar of Companies, Companies House, Crown Way, Maindy, Cardiff CF4 3UZ – you can ask your solicitor to deal with this for you. (Details required are the company's registered office, particulars of shareholders, directors and company secretary.)

FOUR CASE HISTORIES

Let us look now very briefly at how four different people started up in business, and how those critical first 12 months went.

_____

1. John Phillips is a graphic designer in Peacehaven in Sussex. He set up a year ago and after a few months his wife gave up her job and joined him, then a few months ago he took on a full-time employee. When he set up he thought he would be spending 95 per cent of his time on the drawing board and only 5 per cent of the time out getting work and dealing with customers. In fact he has found that he spends only about 50 per cent of his time at the drawing board, with the other 50 per cent spent looking for work, delivering it, checking it over with clients, and dealing with clients on the telephone. His wife now runs the administrative side of the business, does the invoicing, billing, tax, National Insurance and so on, and he has had to employ a full-time graphic artist who spends all his time at the drawing board.

2. Sandra Gardiner is from Ripon in North Yorkshire. She thought she spotted a gap in the market a year ago, noting that there were a lot of self-employed businessmen in the area, many of whom needed perhaps a few hours of secretarial help a week. However, they could not afford and did not need a full-time secretary. She looked around and found that there was no secretarial agency offering this sort of service, so she set up a business offering secretarial services to businessmen. She started off by making herself known through the local Federation of Small Businesses branch, the local National Farmers' Union branch, the Chamber of Commerce and other similar organisations, explaining that her services were available and that they were specially geared to the local small businessman. The work has come in and she has not needed to advertise or do anything more. Sandra considers that a good job delivered on time and well done means that she gets more work by recommendation.

3. Richard Reynolds from Lewisham, in South London, went into the army when he was 15 and eight years later came out as a fully trained mechanic. He had always wanted his own small garage but he did not rush into it. First, he spent a year working for another small garage. Although he already knew how to repair, restore and maintain cars, he did not know anything

Partnership - a two-way commitment

The market potential for Floor Coverings International is substantial. On average, people in the UK and Ireland change their carpet every six years. Every year, more than one and a quarter million people move house, and most re-carpet. Approximately 185,000 new homes are built every year In fact the floor coverings market in the UK and Ireland is worth an estimated £2 billion per year For franchisees, the Floor Coverings International shop-at-home concept offers a means of earning a share of this market.

Yet while a Floor Coverings International franchise is a genuine opportunity to build a thriving business selling directly to receptive consumers, it is important that prospective franchisees understand what is required of them as partners.

Franchisees need to be enthusiastic and dedicated and to have a sound head for business. As well as recognising the exciting opportunity that exists you must have the drive and ability to exploit it. This means business planning is essential. The business plan you put together will indicate your calibre and help you think through the implications of what's involved. It will project what level of income you need to generate and show you what's required to achieve it.

Selling is obviously a key part of the business; but it is not the only part. Franchisees must be able to exercise the disciplines and control associated with any small business: controlling costs, keeping accurate, up-to-date records and monitoring how the business is progressing on a day-to-day basis. Above all, you must quickly become a competent project manager.

The skills you will need include sales and marketing, communications, problem solving, accountancy, people management and customer care.

To help you, all Floor Coverings International franchisees receive a significant level of central support. You are part of a franchise network with access to expertise in many areas. Floor Coverings International is committed to minimising the risks to its franchisees, working with you to help ensure mutual prosperity. Although franchisees should be proactive self-starters, Floor Coverings International will provide you with a wide range of management and marketing tools. One of these tools is a lap-top computer with state-of-the-art software programmes designed to facilitate and develop the business. Indeed, use of new technologies is a key feature of the Floor Coverings International approach.

For further information, please contact:
Floor Coverings International
High Quality House
Sandbeck Way
Wetherby
West Yorkshire

Tel: 01937 588 456
Fax: 01937 584 454

Leading the way...

in home shopping.

about running a small garage. He also spent that year considering how he would make his service different from that of all other small garages. He decided to concentrate on repairing and restoring old sports cars, since he thought that in London and the South East there was a market for such a service. He found that setting up always costs more than you think. He also considers that it is important to keep on top of the book work. He closes his garage at noon on Saturday and spends the whole of the afternoon on his books and does not leave the garage at the weekend until they are completed. His tip is, don't go planning your holidays just because you had a good week, because next week the turnover will probably be poor.

4.   Alex James, again from North Yorkshire, was in middle management in Harrogate, but he attended a 'Be Your Own Boss' seminar and decided to become self-employed. His business is the collection and same-day delivery of small parcels – documents and valuable items – throughout North Yorkshire. After nearly a year he has two vehicles. He advises new entrepreneurs not to rely on promises of work in the early stages. In the first three months he went round all the companies he knew in the area and many of them said, 'Oh yes, Alex, you set up and we are sure that we will be able to find you lots of work.' So he started up, and went back, but all those promises disappeared. People began to say: 'Come back in a fortnight; we haven't got anything this week, but maybe next week.' And for the first three months he spent 95 per cent of his time just knocking on doors to get the work. He had not envisaged that happening; it was not in his cash-flow forecast. At the end of those three months it was touch and go whether he would survive. Fortunately, the work started coming in and all his personal calls began to pay off. Now it is the other way round. He spends 95 per cent of his time on the road and only 5 per cent looking for business. Just the occasional leaflet drop around the area is now enough to ensure continued business.

WHAT MAKES AN ENTREPRENEUR?

So what sort of qualities do self-employed people need? They have to be healthy, persevering, enterprising, hard-working, unflappable, motivated, confident and independent. If you are going to be self-employed you have to be the sort of person who can cope with a bank manager ringing up in the morning telling you that you have gone over your overdraft limit again. You have to be able to handle irate customers and cope with the VAT or Planning Officer coming in and bothering you at the same time, and be able to get on and do your business as well. If you feel that you will not be able to cope with such stress, then self-employment is not for you.

The first quality noted in the list above was health. As mentioned earlier, the DSS and National Insurance are none too generous as far as self-employed people go, and so good health is essential. Government statistics show that for every ten days the typical employed person is ill, a self-employed person is ill for only three days. If you are self-employed, you will probably work much longer hours in much tougher circumstances. If you are the sort of person who is not very healthy, with a long record of sickness, then perhaps opening a shop every morning at 8 am and staying open until 6 pm is not for you.

Being self-employed is a risky business and nine out of ten people who set up in business this week will not be running that same business in five years' time. That does not mean that 90 per cent will have gone bankrupt. There are hundreds of reasons – from emigration to death – to explain why a business will not be running in five years' time. There might be the odd business which is obviously going to run into deficit and so is closed down before its owner goes bankrupt. But people do end up losing the roof over their heads with their houses being put up for sale to pay off their debts, so think very carefully before risking everything in business. If you are still determined, despite all the warnings and potential hazards, then you are advised to do all your homework first so that you go into business with your eyes wide open.

Checklist: What kind of business?

- ☐ Have you assessed the size of the total market and how it is divided amongst your competitors?
- ☐ Are your sales projections realistic and can they cope with variations in the market?
- ☐ Seek out advice to make sure that you have the legal right to produce and sell your product.
- ☐ If you are operating as a sole trader but not under your own name have you displayed the ownership of your business on three places ie: receipts, letters and invoices?
- ☐ Have you had a partnership agreement drawn up by a solicitor?
- ☐ Consider new insurance policies to cover you for ill health and obtain a number of quotes from your broker.
- ☐ If you are considering setting up a limited company seek out advice from your solicitor to help draw up the legal documentation.
- ☐ Consider your health and whether you are able to withstand long working hours associated with working for yourself.

2 What Types of Capital are There?

This chapter is not only about types of capital, but also about some of the principal factors you need to take into consideration in deciding how to finance your business. The following chapter on 'Presenting your case' will guide you through some tried and tested routes.

In financing a small business or raising capital for a new one, you will encounter contrasting viewpoints. Ambitious entrepreneurs need the courage of their convictions, and one of those convictions may well be the infallibility of their idea or project. In other words: 'The banks and other lending establishments should put their money where *my* idea is!'

Those who are in the business of lending money will shake their heads, knowing that in practice the failure rate is high and that most entrepreneurs underestimate the amount of money they will need in order to develop their business – and fail to learn by their mistakes as they do so. The banks will ask:

☐ How much money of your own do you have?
☐ Who bears the initial risk?
☐ Are you going to put your money alongside our money?
☐ And if your business goes wrong, how far will you be committed personally?

It is worth understanding these two points of view before studying the capital structure of new businesses and the types of capital and their sources. This is because central to the growth of any business will be the support of a lending banker. The lending banker has a relatively uncomplicated ambition: to get the original loan back at the end of its term, while receiving the current market rate of interest on it in the meantime. This does not mean that the loan is risk-free. The banks will share some risk, but will seek to ensure that the risks of a business are fairly shared between its proprietors and its financial backers.

It is not possible to cover in one chapter all types of capital for all types of business. It would take a whole book just to cover sole traders, partnerships and limited companies, and then consider capital for new businesses, development capital for growing existing businesses, and public capital for successful businesses. The assumptions in this chapter are that new businesses need venture capital including equity, that existing businesses are profitable enough to need development capital from the banks and that both these businesses are, by and large, limited companies. In fact, in their very early stages, many businesses are unincorporated – often very sensibly so – and they are almost wholly financed by the proprietor's capital and bank overdrafts. This chapter will tend therefore to be about ideals.

GETTING THE RIGHT CAPITAL

The most crucial consideration for financing a new business is getting the capital structure right at the beginning. There will doubtless be plenty of other crises as a business develops, without starting out with the kind of finance that cannot sustain the inevitable financial setbacks. Chapter 3 is all about assessing and presenting the case to the banks and explains the projections which you should undertake. Those projections should enable bankers and venture capitalists to assess possible ways in which the business may progress, and to judge whether the initial capital is sufficient.

One of the venture capital companies has done some research on the problems of new businesses. Apart from highlighting hopeless management, this research suggests that new manufacturing companies, growing steadily, need cash resources of maybe 25 per cent to 30 per cent of the value of their growing sales in order to finance stocks, debtors (less creditors) and other working capital requirements. If you add to that the capital equipment needed, the initial start-up losses from funding overheads and the product development costs, you may get a severe cash requirement over maybe two or three years. If sufficient capital can be raised in one form or another for the assets of the business, even allowing for initial losses, to be twice the amount which the new business borrows, then that will be more than enough to make sure that further temporary facilities can be arranged to cover any hiccups and delays in cash receipts. The business will then be financially stable.

The problem which faces many small businesses at the outset is under-capitalisation; many lose the confidence of their bankers at their first crisis. It is not the lending banker's job to gamble money on a business which only pays a market rate of interest on the uncertain outcome of a new venture. Those small businesses are the first ones to fail.

PROPRIETOR'S CAPITAL

Any business should make sure that it starts life with an adequate base of risk capital. A significant part of that will be the proprietor's capital. Backers, whatever form they take, are more inclined to lend money when they know that the proprietor is doing the same.

There are three sources, at least, for that:

☐ the management – you, the one who wants to start or develop your own business;
☐ external investors (friends, relatives, associates and trading partners);
☐ venture capital companies. The role of private individuals such as business acquaintances who invest in new companies is often overlooked but many enterprises are financed in this way. Such investors are called 'business angels'. There are also some sources of quasi-capital: money which is totally at risk and which will only be paid off if the venture is successful (some government project finance is like that).

The Enterprise Investment Scheme (EIS), successor to the Business Expansion Scheme (BES), is likely to be of more interest now that the Chancellor has added to 20 per cent income tax relief the ability to roll over capital gains tax due from the sale of a previous business or any other business asset. An individual can invest up to £150,000 per year in new shares. With 60 per cent tax relief from these sources, entrepreneurs who have made money in other businesses have a big incentive to invest in new ones. Investment through EIS also makes the sale of shares that have been held for five years free of capital gains tax.

The rules relating to eligibility for EIS are complex and professional advice should be sought. Be particularly careful about remuneration for investing directors, and about mixed loan and equity investment. EIS or tax roll-over relief can be lost if errors are made.

The individual can borrow capital, and will usually get tax relief on the interest. Consequently, if they really believe in their venture, it must be rare for the managing individuals to be unable to raise even a modicum of capital as equity share capital.

Then there are the venture capital companies. Each major clearing bank has connections with some of these companies, if it is not connected with one entirely of its own. This form of capital embraces a wide range of potential investments which are not just for high technology companies. The British Venture Capital Association (BVCA), which is based in London, provides a free list of venture capital companies. Venture Capital Report (VCR; see Appendix III) publish a guide to venture capital in the United Kingdom and Europe and also publish a monthly report which details relevant information on small businesses (between five and fifteen per report) who are seeking venture capital. However, it is worth remembering that venture capital is only for businesses which have been incorporated into limited companies.

What venture capital companies will consider doing is financing your business partly with share capital of various types, and partly with loans. If they do a good job they will offset sufficient of the risk which they bear by taking on completely new ventures with the prospect of gain on the few businesses which are successful. This will enable them to offer a high proportion of loan money, and this loan money should be for a sufficiently long term so that the business not only has some financial security for its early years but is still free to finance temporary needs by overdrafts. Sometimes entrepreneurs look on these finance packages as requiring them to 'give away' some of their equity. That seems an unreasonable view since the investment is not just lending, it is sharing considerable risk. The statistics show that most new businesses fail yet few entrepreneurs accept that, as far as the bank or venture capitalist is concerned, theirs could be one of them.

If you structure the finance of a business properly it will have a greater chance of enabling you to share in most of the prosperity brought by success rather than being left – along with the creditors – with 100 per cent of failure.

A venture capital company will probably draw up a shareholders' agreement which will further ensure that the business is managed in its interests and that it shares in any profits.

DIFFERENT KINDS OF SHARES

The equity in the business may be composed of various types of shares.

Ordinary shares

First, the simple ones. This is typical for each share: one equal amount subscribed, one vote, one equal right to any declared dividend or to the capital of the business. There are all sorts of variations on such ordinary shares. The management's ordinary shares might have dividend rights deferred until a certain participation in profit has gone to the other shares. All those other shares, owned by the venture capitalist, might have a right to a special dividend if profits exceed a certain level.

As the company's worth increases, so does the value of each share held. It is worth noting, however, that should the business fail, borrowed money will have priority for repayment, and both the Inland Revenue and HM Customs and Excise will take what is owed to them before shareholders have a chance of getting anything back.

These are all 'sweeteners' to persuade the investor to provide finance with less of a stake in the equity than if his equity stake had only the same rights as everyone else's. Although this seems quite a good idea, to avoid the feeling of 'giving away' too much of the equity, be careful: if the business is a success it is going to be quite expensive to buy back these shares from the investor who has special profit-sharing rights – even though he did enable the business to get started in the first place.

In businesses where there are sole traders or partnerships, the equity represents any capital introduced plus profits still held in the business.

Preference shares

Preference shares usually carry a fixed cumulative dividend that is paid before ordinary shareholders receive dividends, hence the term 'preference'. However, they usually have restricted voting rights and may not participate in the capital growth of the business. They may be redeemable at some time in the future. The rights attached to them may vary widely, and so some financiers will view them as debt and others as part of the equity capital of the business. For a lending bank, the key question is whether the dividends have to be paid, like interest on a loan. Since preference shares are unsecured, ranking behind debt, a lender will usually view them as equity as long as payment of dividends depends upon the ability of the business to afford them.

WHERE TO LOOK FOR LOANS

There are three types of loan, best described by the length of time they are available: long-, medium- and short-term loans.

Long-term loans

Generally speaking, long-term loans (ten years or more), for use as equity capital, are not provided by the clearing banks but are available from other institutions or some subsidiaries of the clearing banks. Banking prudence, and the principle of matching their sources of funds with their assets, mean that clearing banks very rarely lend longer than ten years, unless under a special contract – five to seven years is more usual.

Long-term loans are more likely to be provided by insurance companies, pension funds, building societies, 3i (Investors in Industry) and the institutions which provide industrial property mortgages, many of whom are also connected with insurance companies. These lenders are looking for a high running yield (high return) on the funds, either because they need that income to meet payments – as the pension funds do – or because that matches the type of finance which they have raised. They require a debenture to secure their loans. If you have a proven track record in running your business it might be possible to negotiate with the lending institution on the matter of how that debenture ranks against the bank, that is, who gets paid first if your enterprise fails. An understanding institution that is prepared to consider a package of loan and equity capital in which the loan is subordinate to an element of bank lending can be a marvellous support to a growing business, but do not expect such support if you have not yet proved yourself.

Contractual term loans are formalised by a specific agreement to cover a specific purpose, period and repayment programme – which might match a cash flow of a project.

Medium-term loans

Medium-term loans are much more home ground for the banks. Every bank has some form of development loan scheme providing five- or seven-year money. Most have some sort of start-up loan scheme by which they will lend money to new businesses, and hope to recover their money and make some sort of extra gain from those which are successful. Most banks also have asset loan schemes for specific purchases.

The cost of schemes, if they involve equity options or royalties, may be difficult to quantify, although in general the banks will want to charge the equivalent of between 3 and 5 per cent above base rates on the money lent.

The cost of more conventional medium-term finance may be slightly less, and the banks will generally look for security in the form of a fixed or floating charge over the company's assets. A commitment fee is usually charged and the borrower is required to pay any costs.

External shareholders, who have a stake in the capital of the business will often provide loan capital as well, possibly linked to a right to acquire more shares in the business.

Instalment credit (hire purchase, in colloquial terms) and leasing have a major application in financing the fixed assets of businesses. Leasing will be the more effective method if taxable profits are not yet anticipated. Instalment credit has now been extended to cover stocking finance for certain industries where the stock items are identifiable. Most leasing companies will demand personal guarantees from directors of new businesses unless the asset that is leased provides very strong security.

When doing your cash flow calculations, remember that leasing companies often charge three months rental as a deposit. There are also items, such as software, that they may decline to finance. Most of the banks have their own leasing companies.

Short-term loans

Factoring provides sales accounting and debt collection services, and sometimes an element of protection against bad debts; usually some 80 per cent of the debts due to the business is receivable immediately and the balance, less charges, is paid when the debt is recovered. There is a range of other discounting services which may not involve managing the sales accounting. They tend to be a little expensive but can relieve the business of time and trouble. They can also, by chasing your debts for you, reduce your administrative costs and your cash tied up by debtors.

If you are embarking on an export programme (see Chapter 11), then letters of credit, or bills of exchange, can be accepted on the London markets and your bank will be able to do this for you.

Revolving credits are rather like household budget accounts, but for companies.

The cheapest form of borrowing is often by the simple overdraft. 'Blue chip' companies have frequently enjoyed overdrafts at a margin of 1 per cent above the bank's base rate. Smaller companies usually bear a margin of 2 to 3 per cent, with new companies being charged up to 4 per cent. Do not blindly accept 4 per cent if another bank will offer you 3.5 per cent – change your bank if necessary. Remember, competition between banks also works to your advantage.

Your bank manager may offer you a loan at a fixed rate of interest: if interest rates rise above the rate charged, you are fortunate. However, the reverse can happen. Think very carefully before accepting a fixed rate option.

Interest rates are an emotive subject. Do not devote all your attention to the rate of interest and ignore bank charges. These should be agreed at the same time since they can swamp loan interest and are equally negotiable. Some industry associations have negotiated special terms with banks on behalf of their members. This may provide sufficient reason to join an association. Always ask about 'arrangement fees' and any other charges, such as legal or security fees. They can be substantial so try to reduce them too.

Many bank managers will have nursed along a new small business on nothing more than an overdraft facility supported by personal guarantees. As a minimum consideration, the overdraft facility should be protected by making sure that 'hard core' overdraft borrowing – that is, the lowest level of borrowing beneath which the overdraft does not go at any time in the course of a year – should be financed in some other way. One of the most common mistakes made in financing small business, after getting the overall gearing (ratio of loans and leasing to equity) too high, is relying too heavily on short-term credit. This pushes up the overdraft and extends creditors to such a level that all flexibility is lost.

Remember that an overdraft is 'on call': the bank can withdraw it at any time without having to give a reason.

Try to avoid giving personal guarantees. Start by saying 'No' when these are demanded. As well as putting your home at risk they make it harder to switch to another bank if you are dissatisfied.

GOVERNMENT SCHEMES

Government grants tend to be associated with assisted areas, areas of economic deprivation and so on. 'Why go to the middle of nowhere when you can come to the middle of London?' asks the London Docklands Development Corporation.

The whole emphasis of government aid for industry has changed, and at times the scale of aid is not always appreciated. A government moratorium in 1985 placed new emphasis on a number of government aid policies. But this policy is designed in part to put greater emphasis on job creation and to improve cost-effectiveness.

The assisted areas, as announced on 23 July 1993, are in two tiers: development and intermediate areas. In development areas (DAs) Regional Selective Assistance (RSA) and Regional Enterprise Grants (REGs) for investment and innovation projects are available. In intermediate areas (IAs) RSA and REGs for innovative projects are available; REGs for investment projects are available in a limited number of IAs. Assistance is available to manufacturing and some service industries. RSA is based on the capital costs of a project and the jobs created or safeguarded by it. Grants are not automatic; they are negotiated between the company and the operating department (Department of Trade and Industry, Scottish or Welsh Offices; see page 201 and 206 for addresses).

Grants given are 'the minimum amount necessary for the project to go ahead'. A REG for investment projects is a flat rate grant equal to 15 per cent of fixed project costs (maximum £15,000) available to companies with fewer than 25 employees. It has a simplified application process but applicants must demonstrate a need for assistance. A REG for innovation projects is a flat rate grant equal to 50 per cent of project costs (maximum £25,000) available to companies with fewer than 50 employees which are introducing a new product or process. It has a simplified application process, but applicants must show that there is a technical risk involved in the project.

At the other end of the scale there is the Business Start-up Scheme, details of which are available from the Training and

Enterprise Councils in England and Wales, and the Local Enterprise Companies in Scotland, through Jobcentres. It is directed to individuals: the main requirements are that you have been unemployed, that you are in receipt of unemployment benefit, and that you have some start-up capital to put into the company, partnership, co-operative or as a sole trader. Under the old scheme (Enterprise Allowance) an allowance of £40 per week was payable for up to 52 weeks to supplement the income of a new business. Now, however, the size and duration of the allowance is more closely tied to each particular enterprise. The sum can range from £20 to £90 a week and be given over a period varying from 26 to 66 weeks. But before you decide whether to apply, go and talk to your tax consultant, as certain tax disadvantages might be brought out regarding your own particular situation should you be a sole trader or in a partnership. The Training and Enterprise Councils also administer funds that may help with staff training or even business planning for new and established companies. Since each of the TECs has different schemes and levels of funding available, it is important to check what your local TEC has to offer.

The Enterprise Fund, which was introduced in December 1998, also makes provision for public and private sector financing to small and medium-sized firms. The four elements of the fund are:

☐ small-firms Loan Guarantee Scheme;
☐ venture capital support for high-tech business;
☐ support for small equity investments (those up to £0.25 million);
☐ the Department of Trade and Industry's 'challenge' to finance industry to come forward with innovative proposals.

The main method of delivery assistance through the Enterprise Fund is via the Loan Guarantee Scheme.

This is a form of selective assistance whereby the government guarantees loans to encourage banks and other financial institutions to lend to small firms that lack security or track record. For new business, or start-ups, the guarantee is 70 per cent on loans of between £5,000 and £100,000. For firms which have been established for two years or more the guarantee is 85 per cent on a maximum loan of £250,000. The borrower has to pay the government a premium of 1.5 per cent on variable interest rate loans and 0.5 per cent on fixed interest rate loans.

Before offering a Loan Guarantee Scheme loan, lenders must satisfy themselves that they _would_ have offered conventional finance but for lack of security. They should establish that all available assets have been used for conventional loans. No personal assets or personal guarantees can be taken as security for the loan. _It is the lender's decision whether or not personal assets are available to be used for conventional lending._ However, the borrower may be required to pledge premises, machinery and other possessions in connection with the businesses as security for the guaranteed loan. The lender will usually take a fixed or floating charge over such assets.

Another government scheme, available through the Department of Trade and Industry, is that of part-contribution towards the cost of export market research. For companies, the contribution can be up to 50 per cent of either eligible costs of the companies' own in-house research or consultancy fees, up to a maximum contribution of £20,000; for trade associations the contribution can be up to 75 per cent of costs incurred on the first application, then a reducing percentage for subsequent applications.

Only companies employing fewer than 200 people may apply for grants for export market research and they must not have made three or more successful applications since 1 January 1986.

The scheme is administered by the Association of British Chambers of Commerce (address in Appendix III).

Another source of finance can be obtained at interest rates well below those of the market. These loans are available from some high street banks, using funds provided by the European Coal and Steel Community (ECSC). Primarily, these loans are for existing manufacturing companies although certain service businesses may also qualify. The aim of the project is to create jobs in areas where high unemployment has occurred in the steel and coal industry. The loans must be secured by a bank guarantee or equivalent security. An ECSC loan can represent up to 50 per cent of the fixed asset element of the project. There is an upper limit per project of £5 million. Loans are usually for periods of five to eight years and the commencement of repayments can often be deferred. When applying to them, the banks ask for a full business plan – including five years' historic accounts – together with profit and cash flow forecasts.

OTHER GRANTS

Some local authorities provide grants to assist established businesses. While this does not directly assist a start-up, the finance may all be part of taking the business through its early development. It is worth contacting your local authority to find out what help might be available for marketing or business development. In addition, funding is available through local Training and Enterprise Councils for training. Contact your local TEC directly or your local Business Link. The Business Link organisations co-ordinate the provision of information on grants and other assistance. They can, themselves, often provide subsidised training.

CAPITAL STRUCTURE

There is a plethora of types of capital for small businesses, and all too often the wrong approach is used in the search for finance – to attempt to raise as much loan finance as possible with minimal personal commitment. The banks and the institutions know by experience that a high proportion of new businesses fail quickly and that most businesses will need more funds than the entrepreneur asks for. It is therefore wise to set out to find the right capital structure. Once you have decided upon the right type of capital which is available to meet your requirements, the next chapter shows you how to present your case to obtain it. Having received some form of finance, we will then show you the sort of records you need to keep and how to monitor and control your business.

Checklist: What types of capital?

☐ Have you identified how much of your own money you are able to invest in the company and if you are prepared to risk it if the business goes wrong?
☐ Consider sources of risk capital and make realistic projections of how much your business will need to get going.
☐ Consider whether you should issue ordinary shares or preference shares.
☐ Identify what type of loan is suitable for your business and what type of organisation should be approached ie: banks, insurance companies, factors.
☐ Contact the Department of Trade and Industry for information on government support.

3 Presenting Your Case for Raising Capital

There are many reasons why you may be wanting to raise capital. If your business is just starting up, or has not been going very long, then you will need to make a presentation for venture capital, possibly to private investors known to you, or to institutional investors who are actively interested in helping to finance the very small business which needs an injection of equity and long-term capital. Or we might be talking about development capital, project capital, or a package of equity and loan capital to help in the acquisition of an existing successful business, or we could be talking about negotiating a management buy-out. Finally, we might be presenting a carefully argued case for UK government or EU finance. In all these examples we are talking about making a presentation. Whatever your specific case, this chapter covers the general principles you need to know for making a presentation about your company.

HOW MUCH CAPITAL IS REQUIRED?

A healthy profit forecast does not necessarily mean that little capital will be required. Some of the biggest demands on capital are:

- [ ] launching and other preliminary expenses;
- [ ] the cost of equipment and premises (sometimes including a premium on leasehold premises);
- [ ] the cost of financing stock, work-in-progress and debtors, after allowing for credit granted by suppliers ('working capital');

☐ sales falling significantly short of expectations, and other deviations from the original plan.

A word of warning when preparing the budget. There is always the risk that sales will be slow to reach expectations, or even that they will not reach them at all. It is therefore important to make sure that adequate capital is available to cover any reasonable shortfall in profits, and it is strongly recommended that profit and cash projections are prepared to reflect the worst envisaged sales income as well as the most likely sales income. An increase in your sales also has to be financed as it means, for example, that you will have to purchase more raw material; you may also have an increased wage bill, as well as other extra costs. These higher costs will generally have to be paid before your customers pay you, leaving a period when you will have to finance the extra costs. When businesses grow faster than they are able to finance this timing difference it is called 'over-trading' and can lead to the bankruptcy of profitable enterprises.

In your cash forecast you should include all items where sums for goods or services are received or paid for at the time of receipt or when the payment occurs. It is different from the trading and profit/loss account which does not deal with any investment you may make and which assumes all is paid in and paid out for a year's business irrespective of the exact timing. In the cash forecast 'capital' items such as equipment and lease premiums as well as pre-trading expenditure must be included. Listed below are some items which have a significant impact on cash forecasts and should therefore be borne in mind:

☐ the proportion of sales on credit and the expected credit period;
☐ the terms of credit, affecting both purchases and sales;
☐ staffing levels and the timing of changes;
☐ upgrading accommodation or equipment as the business expands;
☐ the nature of timing of capital injections.

The cash forecast should cover the same period as the profit projection, showing projected monthly movements for the first year.

It will give you an indication of:

- [ ] the maximum capital requirement (before allowing for interest, which will be dictated by the type of financing deal eventually negotiated);
- [ ] the month in which the maximum requirement will arise;
- [ ] the pattern of the capital requirement (useful to establish the timing of injections and repayments of capital, and the form of finance most suitable);
- [ ] the impact on the capital requirement of slower than expected sales progress.

Remember that the exact timing of receipts and payments is crucial for a new business. If receipts are a week late and payments are demanded a week early, life can become very uncomfortable. Factors such as precisely when VAT or NI becomes payable or when the rates bills arise can be very important to get right.

What is the capital required for?

If the evidence gained from your forecasts suggests that much of the capital will be invested in assets on a medium- to long-term basis (say, for at least two years), then short-term sources of capital such as a bank overdraft or a temporary loan should not be considered. The components of the capital requirement should be analysed to establish what the fund will be used for and therefore the timescale of the financing required. As a general rule it is best to consider longer-term capital unless dealing with, for example, a business requiring virtually no investment in fixed assets (i.e. equipment and premises), and only modest finance for working capital which fluctuates and can be financed by an overdraft.

Your end objective: a bankable proposition

Most businesses ultimately survive, or not, on the strength of the continuing confidence of their bankers. All other financial dealings must result in a bankable balance sheet. If you insist on proceeding against the better judgement of your bank manager, you will risk edging your business that much closer to the appointment of a receiver.

The funding of the business should be sufficient and stable enough to enable it to survive a conceivable period of misfortune. Until that position is reached the business will be fragile, and investors and bankers are likely to take a cautious view. Expansion will certainly require finance for more working capital; so will misfortune. Without an adequate equity base you may have no leeway.

SEEING IT FROM THE OTHER SIDE

This is all about seeing ourselves as others, such as bankers and investors, see us. It is often extremely difficult for smaller entrepreneurs to look at their position critically; they are sure they are right – and very often they are – but nobody will be convinced by assertions. This is where your accountant comes in, who can help you to get an objective view of yourself and your business and should be the person who understands what you are currently engaged in. *Present your business as others want to see it.* To do that you are going to have to anticipate your needs: *anticipation* and *control* should be the two themes of your presentation. A banker wants to see an application which anticipates what might happen, both the worst and the best, and what you plan to do about it, the information you gather and how you use it and how you demonstrate your ability to control the business. Your anticipation and contingency planning feed through into the financial picture the report paints and reflects your management ability. A potential backer will also need full details of the business, from machinery to personnel to sales potential. Make sure that all this information is in a readable form. Your story is exciting – make sure you bring that out and don't make it sound dull.

Many small businesses fall into the trap of being wildly optimistic with their sales projections while forgetting whole areas of cost, leading them to raise too little money for too short a term. Professional advice can be a very good investment.

HAVE YOU GOT A BALANCED MANAGEMENT STRUCTURE?

Before we discuss the finance of your prospective business in detail, we need to take a look at the management, i.e. you and your partners. The question to ask yourself is whether you and/ or your partners or fellow directors have the necessary management expertise for running a business of the kind you hope to start. Take a good look at the experience you can offer between you, and ask yourself whether it is relevant to your proposal. Remember, others will ask these questions about you.

MAKING AN EFFECTIVE PROPOSAL

The picture you must present is of the whole business, warts and all. The points which need to be included in any proposal are listed below:

- [ ] description: physical factors, a broad picture of its operation, factors which might strain, limit or influence operations (e.g. space, plant and machinery, trained personnel);
- [ ] the product, its market and its place in that market, even for a corner shop;
- [ ] competitors and your advantages over them;
- [ ] its base maintainable performance: the level of activity above which you hope to rise but below which there is a very limited danger that you will fall;
- [ ] its track record: trading, not statutory, accounts;
- [ ] what factors affect trading, and how;
- [ ] management's ability and credentials.

Put the detail in schedules or appendices so that the opening is brief, and simply portrays the present business. Always remember to set out just the important factors at the beginning. These two maxims are worth remembering: first, *attention starts to wander after four pages*, and secondly, *you may not be there in person to add your explanations*. Your proposal may have to live and fight alone at some area office or bank committee meeting. If you discover that your bank manager will be passing on your proposal to someone else to deal with, find out who it will go to and send it to him yourself.

Sound business

Your banker is going to want to know some very simple things, such as – is the business sound? It is, therefore, important that you really substantiate your base maintainable profit.

Present your case as others will want to see it, and unless you have financial training and are skilled at financial presentations, turn to your accountant to present an objective case. Take a critical look at your business and its future, just as the banker will do. How much? How long? What if? How do I get it back? These are the questions to be answered. Your presentation should be lucid, logical and frank.

Making assumptions for the future

You should follow your description of the proposition with a careful analysis of the assumptions for the future. Your case is made or broken on the validity of your assumptions and their root in practical business probability. It is vital to get a grip on the essential assumptions about your business, and then put the essence of them across succinctly to your bankers. If they do not understand from your presentation what it is that is crucial to the success or failure of your proposal, and why and how that success or failure comes about, then you will have failed. 'When in doubt do nowt' is a banker's motto. Do not blame the bank manager – blame your presentation.

One can say, cynically, that your crucial assumptions will be those very reasons you will give as excuses when the project collapses: continuing economic recession, poor market launch, high rates of interest, high wage inflation, lack of skilled labour, cheap imports. All the things which made it not your fault that the project collapsed are the things which should have been properly tackled in your initial assumptions. Some areas for assumptions are:

- [ ] the economy of the country;
- [ ] volume of trade: your market;
- [ ] seasonality;
- [ ] personnel;
- [ ] fixed assets and capacity;
- [ ] inflation;
- [ ] the competition;
- [ ] pricing;
- [ ] conclusions from market research;
- [ ] interest rates.

Volume of trade is very important. If you want to start a corner shop it is almost impossible to know how many people are going to come in and buy Mars bars. If you are setting up a new factory, it is very difficult to say what the volume of business going through the factory will be. But in both cases you can make a reasonable attempt. You need not go for full-blown market research, but you can estimate the size of the market you can reach, how much you can sell against the competition, set it against how much you can produce, and then make some hard judgements. You will probably find some useful statistics in the public reference library. If you take professional advice, make sure you choose an adviser who is experienced in marketing at your level of business, such as a business counsellor or a consultant. Bankers are all too familiar with volume predictions of the type that say 'one item will be sold in the first month, two in the second', and so on. Be realistic; you understand your business and you must convey that confidence and knowledge to the bank.

YOUR FORECASTS

The working schedules at the back of your presentation are its engine-room. Here you will have to set out three essential schedules with supporting working papers, which stretch forward over the duration (recommended two- to three-year period) of the required finance:

1. Profit and loss: split between the composition of trading gross profit and overheads.

2. Cash flow: showing as a separate line the contribution from trading before finance and capital items.
3. Balance sheets: including leased assets and leasing liabilities.

Make it clear how the forecasts were arrived at. The assumptions should flow naturally into the profit projections. Some further analysis will help your lender with the answer to 'What if?' Any reader of your presentation should be able to import an assumption of his own and form a view of the impact of that on your business – where, how and with what consequence.

KNOWING YOUR BUSINESS

It is worth pausing here to see what it is that the banker or investor is expecting from the presentation that you have prepared so far. They want to understand your business, but they also want to see that *you understand your business*. Most small businesses are too busy running their concerns and pursuing new ideas either to notice what is happening or to explain objectively what it is they have done and what it is they are really going to do. Your lender will also be looking for evidence of competent financial control – evidence that you are where you are knowingly. Many firms believe that any form of planning is a waste of time, but cash forecasting and the discipline of matching plans to resources do not have to be elaborate and have often proved vital. Finally, your lender will be interested in three particular banking concepts: matching finance to its use, gearing and security. All three should be considered together.

Matching finance

When putting together a presentation it is very important not to be tempted to leave the business that you know about and start playing in the business of money. The most common mistake is to attempt to finance long-term assets with short-term money, and to argue on the hope that increasing property values are going to make an otherwise not very sensible level of borrowing turn into a profitable venture for you.

Any good, small business accountant keeps in touch with the banks and the lending institutions and has a feel for the way they are thinking. One of the things that your accountant should do, apart from converting your 'back of the envelope' ideas into an effective presentation, is to insist that your presentation brings out the financial stability which follows from your proposals. Broadly speaking, this means that long-term investment should be funded with long-term money, and readily leasable assets can often be leased at attractive interest rates and over most of their useful lives. Finance for a particular project or asset should be repaid out of the proceeds generated by the business on that project or asset. Do not try to finance one project by the proceeds of another; the road to ruin is paved with plans for cross-funding. Overdrafts should be limited to working capital requirements, and should be self-liquidating as part of the trading cycle. The cash-flow and profitability projection should be carried forward so that it can be demonstrated that debt finance is repaid out of cash generated by the project. If that cannot be done, then you probably ought to look for longer-term institutional money.

Gearing

The banker will be interested in three forms of gearing. The first concern is the gearing that emerges from your balance sheet. In the past a banker's norm has been one-to-one capital gearing; in other words, the bank puts in a pound for every pound you either put in originally or have retained in the business. (Bankers will often say that they prefer this 1:1 gearing ratio; a climb past a 2:1 ratio is often indicative of a banker's concern, in direct proportion to the extent of the climb.) The ideal approach is to demonstrate that even a higher level of gearing initially will correct itself back to a comfortable norm, without relying on crocks of gold.

The second concern is income gearing. It shows to what extent the cash flow of the business (generally, profits plus depreciation – that is, cash from trading) covers the repayment of finance, interest and leasing costs.

Finally there is operational gearing, which relates to the proportion of fixed costs in the business. If this is high then only a small drop in sales can turn large profits into large losses.

Security

The banker is also interested in security, but is much more interested in minimising the risk than in realising security. Trying to realise a second charge or second mortgage is fraught with problems. No banker wants this type of situation to arise. They are much more interested in the proposition which indicates that there is very little risk; after all, bankers do not like putting receivers in or ending up with fleets of tankers or corner shops.

Forecasting for the future

Here you have a choice: you can forecast in 'current-year' pounds, or you can forecast in 'inflated' pounds. If you use the former method – which is preferred by some people working on very large projects – you have a series of inflation differentials that are shown in a curious way, since they are real rate differences expressed in today's money. If you choose the latter method, you take inflation as one of your assumptions and take a view of wage increases and cost increases, and set all these out quite clearly.

A more complex matter is how you predict interest rates. It is wise not to base a business case on any assumption that interest rates will fall in the future.

Finally, it is amazing how many people put forward projections in which they have wholly overlooked some physical bottleneck or some manual or executive difficulty in actually getting that volume of activity within the timescale. Negotiations either with labour forces or with central or local government are in the forefront of such problems.

FINDING THE RIGHT FINANCE

Chapter 2 has guided you through some of the different types of capital available, and this section aims to emphasise the importance of selecting the right kind of finance, and to help you to do this successfully.

For the smaller business, directors' guarantees – usually supported by a charge over personal assets – are generally called for. While efforts to resist this are worthwhile, you may not succeed. The banks consider such guarantees necessary because the directors have all the assets under their effective control and the bank wishes to see that the management is totally committed. As to the security offered by the business, you might find that you can borrow up to 80 per cent of property valuations – depending on the location and the economic climate. Debtors can be factored, but a bank may go most of the way to meeting working capital. However, their security valuation of your stocks and debtors will depend on your specific business.

The longer the term of finance you require, the more expansive the presentation. This is because the medium-term assumptions become more and more important and there is more to build on any established track record.

It is worth stressing here that a viable project with good management does not necessarily succeed in raising finance. It is a widely held view of entrepreneurs that the trouble with this country is that the banks are too unimaginative and our financial institutions too rigid and dominated by security for business proposals to get off the ground. However, considerable finance is available and is keenly seeking good and clearly explained projects, acquisitions, ventures and buy-outs in which to invest.

This section is by no means definitive as there are other ways of raising capital. As we have stressed many times before, unless you are familiar with financial arrangement and control, get yourself a good accountant. After all, he or she is not only qualified to deal with such matters, but should also be fully aware of the opportunities which are available.

SHOPPING AROUND

In the case of long-term finance you are bound to find that not only will you have to talk about your proposal several times, but that it is also a good idea to arrange a tour of your operation and management for prospective financial backers. If substantial development capital is required, you may well find that the lender, who is effectively becoming the investor, would like some say in the management of your business, usually by representation on the board. Then, of course, you really must shop around. Money is available just like any other commodity. Different people place different prices on the money they have to offer – dramatically so, when looking for leasing quotes. You must shop around not only among lenders of the same type of finance but also between different types of capital. It is nearly always worth getting an opinion from one of the clearing banks – from a lively, enterprising manager local to your business. Sometimes you can go the whole way with a clearing bank; sometimes you will need to move on to a development capital house, venture capital or various institutions. You should not overlook government sources of finance – either from central government or from Europe, or, increasingly, from local government.

So there are seven vital factors for small businesses to remember:

☐ prove the volume of business;
☐ present the case for others to understand;
☐ concentrate on your assumptions;
☐ work through a profit and loss and cash-flow forecast;
☐ provide a series of projected balance sheets;
☐ match the assets and finance you are seeking;
☐ show you can monitor and control your business.

KEEPING INFORMED

Although not strictly part of any discussion about raising capital, installing and regularly reviewing your financial and management information system is not only important for running a business competently, it is also an important aspect of raising capital. Any banker will be delighted to find that you have a management information system which will regularly produce monthly accounts comparing your actual performance with your budgeted performance. Your bank manager will be very interested in a simple monthly package. This can readily be handled on a personal computer (PC), but shop around for a good computer package. Choose a proven system which many accountants are familiar with, rather than looking for the newest, cleverest package. Banks often ask for monthly accounts. You may give them abbreviated information or you may feel that this is too much trouble and give them what you have got.

Cash crises

It is relatively rare that one can be relaxed about cash crises, and these crises can happen whenever a business is thinly capitalised and expanding quickly. There is only a thin line between expansion and over-trading, and over-trading in a business with narrow margins during a time of high interest rates can sometimes tip the scales on a thinly capitalised operation towards a crisis.

It is important to realise that cash crises often have nothing to do with profitability. It is a not uncommon mistake for entrepreneurs to wave their internal accounts demonstrating that production is profitable, while simultaneously failing to see that a lot of the profit is going into stock and that the business is not generating cash.

There is, of course, no substitute for anticipation, so your management information system must be cash-sensitive. That should, in turn, imply that your operations are analysed by product, or outlet, or whatever other flow makes up your business, so that you can identify where the money is made or lost and what it is that contributes most to your costs. It is surprising how few businesses know which decisions involving allocation of resources generate cash and which lose cash. It is, however, a medium-term problem to get decision making right. The short-term solutions are usually to restrict stocks, to work vigorously on debtors, and to defer maintenance and asset purchase either by leasing or renting, or just by ceasing to buy plant and vehicles. Such an organised reduction in the level of activity needs to be handled very carefully. With skill, it can sometimes be achieved with judicious pricing-up. A slightly expensive but perhaps effective proposition might be to factor debts.

Whatever you do, do not tackle the problem of a cash crisis in a piecemeal fashion. It is just as important to present to yourself, to your fellow managers and, maybe inevitably, to your existing or new financial backers, a well-reasoned plan, another presentation if you like, of the agreed action that you intend to take and of the expected results, and then to monitor its achievement.

Some of the most rewarding work for accountants (and for managers and bankers) arises from 'intensive care work' where, through sitting with the company's management, sometimes over a long period, the accountants regain for them the trust and confidence of their bankers, help them pull the company round and nurse it back to health.

Fudged accounts

All too often accountants investigating a company for a client or an investing organisation come across the statement: 'Of course, we are much more profitable than our accounts show us to be. The directors take out £X0,000 in ways other than remuneration. There are lots of assets worth more than is stated in the accounts.'

It is very difficult to sell or finance a business on numbers that cannot be seen and the same applies when trying to impress a potential supplier or customer. Misleading accounts strike at your credibility and general honesty and when you _do_ need money you will have to rebuild that credibility and trust.

QUOTATION

Finally, you may have long-term plans for allowing your shares to be traded, either outside the Stock Exchange through Ofex, or the Alternative Investment Market or through a full listing. You cannot prepare too early if your proposed course includes anything like a prospectus. Your presentation will then start with an accountant's investigation, known as a 'long-form report'. This will review the history of the business, past accounts and accounting policies, and will include a profit forecast and an examination of working capital needs. These investigations are rigorous, and your sponsors will rely on them.

SHOWING COMMITMENT

Make sure that you have a brief synopsis of the age, education and experience of yourself and your partners to prove that you are capable of running the business, and remember that in most cases you will not be present when the final decision is made. Make sure too that the investment and commitment you and your partners have made are clearly shown. Investors and bankers are keen to have security to ensure their money will not be lost. They also seek assurance of the commitment of management to protect a shared investment. Give brief details of your business, the product, its market and the competition. Explain why you are different and why you will succeed. If you are already in business, then show the latest accounts with up-to-date profit and loss as well as borrowing history. Give details of your key personnel, their functions and qualifications, and supply a list of the principal shareholders. Do explain fully the purpose of the business and the market-place in which its products are competing; your presentation will not be complete with just the financial information. Profit projections must be broken down to show costings, project sales, orders held, legal and audit fees. Be factual and state precisely the amount of finance required and what it will be used for, and make sure that your projections include repayments in the cash flow.

Be prepared, and before deciding whom to approach for financial backing, go along and talk it through with your accountant who will be in the best position to advise you on the different types of finance available and, more importantly, the kind of finance best suited to your needs. Be quite clear as to what your proposal will include and what assets are available for security purposes. Finally, it is worth noting that, depending on your own background, a presentation supported by a reputable professional intermediary such as a financial consultant or accountant may be considered in a more favourable light by potential backers, since they will have carried out some investigation. Not least, their experience may help in presenting a better case.

Checklist: Preparing finances

- ☐ Are your health, training, enthusiasm adequate? Have your family and friends agreed to compensate for your weaknesses?
- ☐ Have you drawn up a profit-and-loss type budget?
- ☐ Have you drawn up a cash-flow plan?
- ☐ Have you a business plan set out in writing?
- ☐ Is your potential profit worth all your effort?
- ☐ Is it possible to test the market further before final commitment?
- ☐ Have you checked on sources, quantities, costs, and reliability of material and stock supply?
- ☐ Is your budgeted profitability realistic?
- ☐ Have you registered as a sole trader/partnership or formed a company?
- ☐ Have you had business stationery printed to facilitate purchasing, negotiation, etc and did you receive a number of different quotes for its printing?
- ☐ What minimum accommodation will you need?
- ☐ Have you prepared a sketch of your lay out plan?
- ☐ Have you arranged enough capital?
- ☐ Have you any further reserves (property, cars or other items)?

If you buy an existing business
- ☐ What will you pay for goodwill, fittings, plant, etc?
- ☐ How will you check the stock, debtors, tax debts, redundancy payments, etc. are claimed?
- ☐ Will you insist upon seeing at least three years' audited accounts?

Reproduced by kind permission of the Department for Education and Employment from the Small Firms Service booklet, _Running Your Own Business._

4 | Finding the Right Premises

'There are three things important in property: location, location and location.' For years this has been the golden rule in considering property and indeed, it is as true today as it has always been. However, in recent years occupiers have come to realise more and more the importance of the suitability of a property to their precise requirements in improving work processes, efficiency and profitability. When looking for accommodation, the main thing is to plan as far as possible in advance. It may be that you have certain timescales laid down for you; your lease on existing premises may be coming to an end, or you may have a certain piece of plant on order for which there is a delivery date for installation in your new property. Dealing with property is a complex subject and not all the factors will be under your control, so you need to avoid a mad panic in the last few weeks. Whatever business you are starting and whatever your needs, whether it is a corner shop, an office or a factory, do list precisely what your requirements are before starting your search.

WHAT SORT OF PREMISES DO YOU NEED?

Many questions need to be asked when considering potential properties for occupation and while many will be common to all types of occupier, you will need to consider your own specific requirements as well. However, some of the more general questions that need answering include:

☐ How reliant are you on passing trade?
☐ Are you going to lease or purchase and what price can you afford?

☐ Are irregular shapes acceptable, or must it be rectangular or square?

☐ Are precise dimensions of the property, including height, of prime importance? (eg for accommodating a racking system in a warehouse).

☐ Can you accept pillars or do you need a clear span?

☐ Are you going to have your offices and factory in the same complex?

☐ Is there sufficient capacity of gas, water, electricity and drainage for your needs?

☐ How secure should the property be in order to meet your insurance requirements?

☐ Do you want (and can you afford) a prominent or prestigious building or situation?

☐ How essential is accessibility for your suppliers and your own transport?

☐ If you do have your own transport, are you heavily reliant upon it, and what provisions for parking do you need to make? If not, how accessible are modes of transport such as train services?

☐ Are there adequate waste disposal facilities?

☐ Do you have any other special requirements specifically relating to your business?

☐ Does the prospective property have the necessary planning permission for your use?

☐ Is there likely to be a need for additional floor space in the foreseeable future?

These then are some of the common questions of a general nature that you will need to consider when choosing your premises.

Clearly, where applicable you will want to ensure that transport costs are kept to an absolute minimum. Therefore, it may well be that by siting your property so that access to essential motorways, main roads, airports etc, is convenient you can considerably improve the efficiency and profitability of your company, both in terms of accessibility to markets and in respect of fewer man hours lost by workers stuck in congestion.

If you are starting from scratch, you will obviously want to ensure you can obtain the right skills in your chosen locality. If

CAPITAL BANK leads the way
with flexible mortgages for the
self-employed

Self-employed mortgage specialist, CAPITAL BANK Mortgages Ltd a Bank of Scotland Group company, understands that customers who work for themselves require special help when it comes to taking out a mortgage.

Most lenders are pleased to supply mortgages which suit Mr & Mrs Average but may not take into account the often irregular flow of income and profits that comes with self-employment.

Without the usual PAYE payslips or P60s, self-employed customers have to rely on their accounts to qualify for a mortgage. Most banks ask for three years' audited accounts backed by an accountant's letter. They also may not take into consideration that customers minimise their tax liability by deducting expenses on overheads. This reduces the apparent profitability of the customer's business, which in turn means the amount they are able to borrow falls short of the amount that they need.

In contrast, innovative lender, CAPITAL BANK, always use individual credit assessment. This means that a customer's whole financial situation is taken into account, rather than judged on a narrow set of criteria, and as a result mortgages can often be granted after just one years' trading. CAPITAL BANK assesses customers by taking up bank and tenancy references, existing lender references and carrying out credit checks. CAPITAL BANK's wide range of SELF mortgages are offered at special rates and are underpinned by good service.

CAPITAL BANK recognises that flexibility is the key to the way that many small businesses operate and it is one of the few lenders to make flexible mortgages available to those working for themselves. When business is going well flexible mortgages allow customers to overpa their mortgages whilst maintaining the ability to drawdown money or take a payment break when business is slow. CAPITAL BANK's Fast-Track Direct flexible mortgage is available with an exclusive 0.35% discount APR 6.7 for the life of the mortgage.

Julie and Paul Laverick of Brough in East Yorkshire paid back the cashback from a previous mortgage to switch to a flexible mortgage. Julie Laverick said: 'As a builder, Paul's work is seasonal in nature. So some months we have lots of spare cash and in others we don't. We like the fact that the flexible mortgage lets us either make overpayments without penalty or take a payment holiday.'

For further information on mortgages from CAPITAL BANK, call

0800 783 1204†

Lines open: Mon to Thu: 8.00am - 8.30pm,
Fri: 8.00am - 5.15pm, Sat: 10am - 2pm.

Quoting reference SRYB 0599

CAPITAL BANK

(A BANK OF SCOTLAND GROUP COMPANY)

City House, City Road, Chester CH88 3AN.

you require advice in this direction, then the Department for Education and Employment will be able to provide a great deal of information about the skills available in your area. However, if you are moving an existing business, you will want to be sure that all your workers are willing and able to move to your new location if necessary. Ensure also that the move will not hinder future sales.

Town planning requirements are particularly important, because the property must have planning permission for the use to which you are going to put it. Look very carefully at any conditions that are attached to the planning permission; for example, there may be noise restrictions or restrictions on working hours, which could present very serious drawbacks. If the property does not have planning permission for your purpose, discuss the matter with the local town planning officer. If you do not make any progress, seek professional advice on how to proceed.

If you are a retailer, then clearly you must determine how reliant you are on passing trade. Obviously prime locations attract significantly higher rents which could be out of range for new retailers. In this case you may have to seek the next best thing; a secondary area where the levels of rents are within your grasp, but which is still in an acceptable trading location.

Many new small businesses will be owner occupied. Although not necessarily an investment – the primary concern is running a business – if you buy a property, then you commit a considerable amount of effort and money, and therefore it is wise to ensure when you do come to sell you are able to recoup a large amount of the investment, if not all of it.

The position of competitors will also need to be considered. Many firms, particularly retailers, obviously feel that their turnover will be all the better for a lack of competition in the immediate area. However, many businesses, often of a specialist nature, such as antiques shops, feel that there are benefits to be gained from being situated together as they will jointly benefit from the combined 'pull' of customers. Either way you clearly need to be fully aware of the location of any competition before you move.

The occupation of property incurs several additional costs which can vary significantly depending on the size and nature of your property. For instance, the payment of non-domestic rates is assessed by reference to the rateable value the property which is based upon the rental value of same as at 1 April 1993. However, from the year 2000 the rate will be set upon the rental value at 1 April 1998. Rates are a significant cost of occupation and you will need to ensure that you are able to meet this liability. Similarly, unless you have an internal repairing lease you are likely to find yourself liable for maintaining the property in a good state of repair. Again financial allowances need to be made to accommodate this as indeed you will have to do so to ensure that the building is fully insured.

If you have, or are thinking of, setting up a high-tech business, there are a great number of Science or Business Parks being built throughout the country. These Parks are a relatively new inclusion in Britain and the units are specially designed to assist new small business, treating it as an embryo unit. Common facilities, such as managerial assistance, administration and secretarial work are usually included in the package. In addition to time sharing facilities there are other benefits such as published research, technological expertise and shared expenses on expensive equipment.

Free Ports have also been established and are located in areas of high unemployment in order to assist in the creation of new jobs. There are many Free Port Zones internationally, but in Britain they are unusual. Basically they are small secured areas where duties do not have to be paid on imports until they cross the Free Port Initial Boundary, and duties do not have to be paid on goods exported. There are many advantages in locating a business in a Free Port although there are disadvantages to be borne in mind, such as the additional cost of premises.

Finally, before you decide to move into your new premises – having already calculated in advance the cost of agency fees, as well as solicitors' and other professional fees, petrol, telephoning, removal, time, etc – look around you. Have you considered equipment? How are you going to pay for the furniture and stationery? Have you thought of the cost of getting your letterheads printed? Though you will be able to claim tax allowances for many of these items, make sure that you have planned for these extra costs in your budgets.

HELP IS AT HAND

Currently there are around half a dozen specialist mortgage lenders in the UK which cater specifically for borrowers who find it difficult to obtain loans from the mainstream banks and building societies — either because they have had historical credit problems such as arrears and County Court Judgements (CCJs), or because their circumstances mean they are rejected by conventional credit scoring. For example, newly self-employed applicants may find difficulty in providing evidence of income, because they have not been trading long enough to produce the required amount of audited accounts. These lenders are often termed 'sub prime', 'non conforming' or 'credit impaired'.

Southern Pacific Mortgage Limited is one of the UK's leading lenders in this market. Starting from scratch just over two years ago, SPML now has 70 staff based in South Kensington, and is on target to achieve £250 million of mortgage completions in 1999.

The company offers three main types of mortgage. The 'Standard' mortgage is available to both employed and self-employed applicants and is available at both variable and fixed rates. The 'Let' mortgage is for applicants who want to buy a property to let out to tenants, and the amount which can be borrowed is based on the rental value of the particular property. Private investment in residential property is currently one of the fastest growing areas in UK mortgage lending.

The 'Right to Buy' mortgage is for local authority and housing association tenants who qualify under the Government's Right to Buy scheme. Many Right to Buy applicants require loans smaller than £25,000 ('regulated' loans under the Financial Services Act), as purchase prices are often heavily discounted for long-term tenants. The majority of mortgage lenders do not offer regulated loans, however SPML is equipped to offer them and therefore help borrowers in this area. Applicants are able to borrow a maximum of £20,000 above the discounted purchase price.

All SPML's interest rates are tied to the London Inter Bank Offer Rate (LIBOR), which is reviewed quarterly and any changes to borrowers' rates take immediate effect.

SPML's mortgages are only available through financial advisers, not direct from the company. One of its leading partners is Simpleloans Mortgages. Simpleloans is run by managing director, Mark Young; is based in Lichfield, Staffs; and specialises in sub prime mortgages. Simpleloans deals direct with the public, marketing its services through advertising on Teletext, TV magazines and elsewhere. Mark comments: "SPML brings a high level of understanding to the individual applicants' needs and has the ability and technology to provide a fast-track service, which is often very important to my clients".

For further information please phone freephone on:

0800 052 0475

BUYING OR LEASING?

There are three main types of property ownership in the main: freehold, leasehold and ground lease.

Freehold

Owning the freehold interest in your property means that provided you stay within the statutory law, you can do with it basically what you will. The problem with buying is having to raise the purchase money. For new businesses, commercial mortgages can prove difficult to obtain and therefore close consideration needs to be given to this matter. This is very much the case at present as lenders, wary of having had their fingers burnt as a result of the crash in values in recent years, are very stringent in their vetting of potential borrowers. Additionally, at present mainstream commercial lenders will usually only give advances of up to circa 70 per cent of the purchase price and so a considerable amount of money will be required from other sources if a purchase is to go ahead. You will also have to be sure that your business can generate enough profit to pay the interest on the loan and it is quite likely that the risk capital that you have will give a much greater return if it is employed in the business rather than invested in the property. The level of return expected on premises in the long term is generally much lower than that expected if capital is invested within the business.

If you have been established in business for some time and if you buy a sound property at the right price, it could become a good capital investment over the years. However, in the past when you decided to realise your money from the sale of a commercial property, you found that it had been an excellent hedge against inflation. However, the dramatic fall in freehold values since the start of the decade means that, in many localities throughout the UK, this is no longer the case.

Leasehold

One advantage of leasing is that there is little capital outlay in acquiring occupation of the building. In many cases, it is just a question of fitting out – which you would have to do anyway with a purchased building. The principle of Section II of the Landlord & Tenant Act 1954, together with subsequent amending legislation, is that when your lease comes to an end you have the right to remain in occupation under the terms of a new lease. There are two exceptions to this rule. If you have been a bad tenant, then obviously there are means by which the landlord can get you out. What is slightly more important so far as the tenant is concerned is that if the landlord wants to occupy his own premises for his own purposes, or wants to redevelop, then he can, under certain circumstances, take possession against you. Normally, he will have to pay you compensation on a statutory basis, and this is related to the rateable value and the time that you have been in possession.

If you lease a building, you will sign a tenancy agreement with your landlord in which he ensures to the best of his ability that you are covenanted to look after the property and not to make any alterations or change its use without his approval. There will be other restrictions on what you can actually do to the property, subject to the landlord's consent, accompanied by regular rent reviews. Furthermore, you will not build up any equity in the property; in other words, when you come to dispose of your interest you will, at best, get only a nominal value for it unless a clause in your lease permits you to sell your outstanding lease to another.

Do not consider leasing a space larger than is required for your business, with the intention of sub-letting the extra space. There are strong restrictions on sub-letting and there is the added risk that (in many areas) you may not be able to find a sub-tenant for the extra space and you will still have to pay rent, rates, insurance and maintenance on it until such time as you are successful in doing so.

Always make sure that you know precisely how much you are paying and what you are getting for that amount; this applies particularly to the service charge.

While the landlord has by law to meet statutory requirements when leasing the property, it is the lessee's responsibility to ensure that the premises comply with the Health and Safety at Work Act.

Ground lease

If you are an established business looking to expand, or moving to premises purpose built for your use and processes, then this course of action may be viable. The prospective tenant effectively rents the site on a long-term basis from the landlord at a nominal rent and then builds the factory or other premises as required thereon. Clearly this can be a costly operation although it should be noted that at the present time construction costs remain relatively low. For new businesses, commercial mortgages and other forms of funding may be difficult to obtain and therefore close consideration needs to be given to this matter.

NEW OR EXISTING PREMISES?

Whether you decide to go with new or existing premises will depend upon several factors and once again many of the considerations will be very specific to your own proposed use. For instance, your business may be such that the image it portrays is of key importance, in which case a more modern, clean looking, efficient property may be suitable. On the other hand, if you renovate or store machinery, then something less impressive may suffice.

One advantage of new premises is lower repair and maintenance costs. If the building has been designed correctly and built to the proper standard, then it will require very little attention – certainly for the first five or ten years or so. A new building is more likely to meet modern requirements in terms of thermal insulation, traffic circulation, car parking provisions and so on.

If the building is specifically designed for your purposes it can incorporate your exact requirements, and still leave room for expansion. Furthermore, by the time you have gone through planning permission and had the building designed and built, you can easily find that some 12 months or so has passed, even for the most modest scheme – and considerably longer for something more ambitious. If you are in a hurry, this sort of timescale may not be acceptable.

Another disadvantage of a new building is the high cost of purchasing or renting. In addition, the rateable value of a new building may be relatively higher than older premises.

An advantage of existing buildings is their availability. The number of new buildings on the market at any one time will obviously be far fewer than the number of existing buildings, and therefore there is a much greater choice. Existing buildings are also cheaper although they will have higher maintenance and running costs. It should be remembered that adaptation costs can be surprisingly high if the building has to be altered to suit your business needs – even the most minor work can cost several thousand pounds. Also many older buildings are ill suited for the installation of complex machinery, networked computer systems, air conditioning, three-phase power etc. Moreover, a building that was put up in the 1950s almost certainly will not have thermal insulation to speak of, and so your heating bills are going to be higher than in a modern building.

Most modern industrial buildings are single storey constructions which are more flexible in accommodating manufacturing processes and plant and machinery, but older buildings may not be. Consideration of the floor loading is particularly important to the industrial user and warehouseman and, in view of the new types of office equipment now available, the loading factor is also becoming important for office users. In older buildings this may present a problem which cannot be economically remedied.

Is there sufficient capacity of gas, water, electricity and drainage for your needs? For example, if the building has only a 29 gas supply and you have ordered a new industrial oven that requires a capacity, say, of 49 supply, then obviously you must calculate the cost of putting in the new gas main before you decide to buy the property. Take a look at the condition of the external services, especially in an older building.

Fire officers, the Health and Safety Executive and factory inspectors are becoming stricter all the time, particularly with regard to past construction methods and materials employed therein such as high alumina cement and asbestos. What was acceptable ten years ago will not necessarily be passed today, and you may well be advised to carry out certain improvements. There is also the disadvantage that, if the building is old or in a poor location, it may not hold its value as an investment and may be difficult to sell when you move to a more modern or larger property. It is therefore wise to seek professional advice.

FINDING YOUR PROPERTY

Chartered surveyors and estate agents

Your first port of call should be to contact either a chartered surveyor or a commercial estate agent. There are a number of firms, both large and small, in most towns and cities which deal with the acquisition, sale and leasing of commercial and industrial property, offices and shop premises; you will find them listed in the local directories or, alternatively, you can contact the Royal Institution of Chartered Surveyors (RICS) (Telephone: 0171 222 7000) for further advice and help in finding one. The RICS also produce a helpful publication, *The Business Property Handbook*, at only £5.95.

Furthermore you may feel that you need professional assistance and representation in acquiring a suitable property and again the chartered surveyor or commercial estate agent can perform this role. Find out what service each one can offer and under what terms. Take advice from colleagues with a personal knowledge of the various firms or seek the advice of the RICS before choosing the surveyor or agent who is best suited to your purposes. Brief him about the type of property you require and your price range. He will know what is available in the market and at what price.

As he is acting on your behalf it will be your representative's job to negotiate the best terms for you. However, it is as well to keep yourself informed as to how matters are progressing. Town planning matters, rating and insurance valuations are also dealt with by him and, if you are leasing property, then the surveyor can prepare a schedule of condition prior to occupation, if required. If you are considering development, then planning permission is required and Building Regulations approval needs to be gained, and your representative can again assist you in this.

If you have an existing property to sell, the chartered surveyor or estate agent can advise you on the best method of marketing it, the price to ask, and he can also put it on the market and negotiate the sale. In any case it is advisable to get an independent opinion from a surveyor when purchasing or leasing your chosen property. Your solicitor will scrutinise the terms of the lease or purchase before you sign.

Other sources of information

The vast majority of properties on the market are advertised, so the columns of your local newspaper will also give you a good idea of what is available, as will a number of specialist business space publications, along with property supplements appearing in a number of quality national newspapers. If nothing suitable is apparent, it may be worthwhile placing your own advertisement in a 'Premises Wanted' column. Increasing numbers of chartered surveyors are getting up Internet Web sites which carry details of properties available.

Additionally you may wish to contact the employment promotion units run by local authorities and government agencies. You will find them in the local telephone directory and they are extremely helpful in giving details of premises. Other government authorities will also be very helpful. If you seek a rural location, speak to the Rural Development Commission or a chartered surveyor in a rural practice.

Finally, drive around the desired areas and see what you can find. Not only will this be useful from the point of view of looking for suitable property and getting a feel for the general character of the area, but also to see if any of your competitors are in the immediate area.

Checklist: Finding premises

- ☐ Do you know how much space will suffice for, say, three years?
- ☐ Will you commission an estate agent to help you locate premises for purchase or rental?
- ☐ Does a building to your requirements exist or will alterations need to be made?
- ☐ Have you allowed for good access, adequate height, easy loading, sound ventilation, drainage, etc?
- ☐ Who must you contact about alterations to buildings?
- ☐ Have you sought consent or advice on planning, licensing, health, trade, etc?
- ☐ Have you obtained full and thorough plant and equipment installation details?
- ☐ Have you considered the extent of open, secure or bonded storage?
- ☐ Will you require any special services (three-phase or high-voltage electricity, gas, air, etc)?
- ☐ Are waste disposal facilities adequate?
- ☐ Are covenants within a lease likely to prove restrictive?
- ☐ What else should be considered in your case?

5 Marketing and Sales

WHAT IS MARKETING?

In an uncertain economic climate it is more important than ever that new starters grasp the principles of marketing. People and businesses will still need goods and services but you may need to refocus your strategy and target those areas that are more susceptible. In the last recession, house building, estate agency and removals came to a stop but conservatories and extensions blossomed for the over 50s and the retired who were impervious to mortgage repayments. The rash of building society share issues have spawned surges in overseas holidays, home computers, new cars and financial services: not every sector of society is hurt by an economic downturn.

Astute marketing will encourage you to concentrate on specific areas where you can generate profit.

Get your marketing right and the rest of your business should be relatively straightforward. With a healthy, profitable order book you can approach lenders with more confidence, organise staff and output and sleep easy at nights. Marketing is more than just selling. Marketing is knowing where you want to go. Selling is getting there. It encompasses research, advertising and promotion, public relations (PR), direct mail, packaging and presentation. It is a mixture of management experience, art, common sense, gut feel – and flair. An interest in psychology and motivation helps. Think of all the well-known successful businesses. They tend to be strong on design and innovation, are often aggressive in their market, are well respected and have excellent customer relations.

For new small businesses marketing can be simplified as identifying a need, fulfilling it at a profit and securing repeat purchases. Many products or services will be bought once – the trick is to get people to come back as satisfied customers, and tell their friends.

WORK OUT A STRATEGY

Before committing time and resources you need to think and plan where to direct your efforts. You need an overall marketing strategy that will include:

- [ ] whether you are targeting business or the public;
- [ ] an identifiable market niche (exploit a gap, don't follow the herd);
- [ ] a growth sector with good margins – what are the trends?
- [ ] basic simple research to identify a need and to determine at what price level and potential volume;
- [ ] a target sales forecast for the short- and medium-term;
- [ ] how you intend to research that market (direct sales, agents, advertising off the page, etc).

The strategy will set out some realistic targets in a given timescale and should act as a discipline to prevent you veering off on fruitless chases. The early days will inevitably be a toe-dipping exercise with each venture done in stages before committing yourself to a definite line. Don't be afraid to trial and test while all the while remembering that *profit,* not turnover, should be your goal. It is easy to be a busy fool.

PRODUCT OR SERVICE?

Products are usually easier to market than intangibles (such as providing a service), yet new service businesses outnumber manufacturers (and that includes crafts) by ten to one, probably because less capital is required to start. A product can be handled, loaned on trial and measured against known standards, whereas services are largely taken on reputation and promise. The personal element is all important and the way you approach and handle prospects can make or mar your business. Garages, hairdressers, travel agents, insurance salesmen are all there to spread confidence and knowledge in a highly competitive market. They all want repeat business.

It is important that you sell a service with belief, warmth and integrity: in reality you are selling yourself. What you really have to offer is almost of secondary importance. With no product, your marketing efforts should be directed towards cultivating a thoroughly professional image: stationery, signs, staff training, furnishings – the total environment in which you operate. Judicious use of PR (both internal and external) is needed to maintain a high and confident image. Customer care is of the utmost importance and must include a complete after sales service. Your best advertisement is through word of mouth. You need to develop a style and a personality for the way you run your business that fits your position in the market place.

FIRST DO THE RESEARCH

A common error with new businesses is to set up, replicate and undercut existing competition with little thought on how to survive on a lower price structure. A professional marketing approach will try and *differentiate* your business from the competition – not attack it head on. So market research is needed to first identify:

- ☐ What are the gaps in current supply?
- ☐ Where is the competition?
- ☐ What are consumers looking for?
- ☐ How can you fulfil that demand profitably?
- ☐ How can you economically promote to that target audience?
- ☐ Is the market growing or shrinking?
- ☐ What will you need to increase your share of the market?
- ☐ What is the likely profile of your average customer?
- ☐ Where in the market should you position your product?

The last question may need some explanation as it is central to all your marketing. If you just think about shopping habits, you can divide this nation into those who shop at Sainsbury's and those who swear by the Co-op. Newspaper readers are often fiercely loyal to *The Daily Telegraph* or *The Guardian* and no amount of price manipulation will shift that loyalty, as recent price wars have shown. There is more to buying a product than just price. These papers have each positioned themselves to attract a certain type of reader who has a different outlook on life, spends their salary in different ways – and of course votes for a different party.

Your product should be no different. Positioning governs the tone of voice with which you advertise, package and price; even the quality of letter-heading that you use. It is the total image with which you speak to the public and this must be borne in mind throughout all your marketing decisions.

BUSINESS OR CONSUMER?

Your own background and experience may well decide whether you deal purely with business or the public. In some cases it is easier to deal solely with the trade – less paperwork, fewer and larger accounts and probably easier identification of the users. Companies tend to be more stable and can be tracked down by the multitude of sources including *Yellow Pages*, trade directories and magazines, exhibitions and mailing lists. Be careful not to become too dependent on one outlet and watch your credit control. If you straddle both sectors a careful price structure needs to be established.

FIND THE SEGMENT

Small businesses survive by selling to a selected part of the market, not by trying to cover the whole. The traditional grocer has disappeared into the clutches of the supermarkets but a delicatessen may survive if it stocks exotic or ethnic foods and is in the right location – it services a distinct sector of the market. Few garages now sell tyres and exhausts – that need has been picked up by the 'quick-fit' service centres. Mail order lends itself well to the specialist segment, from say jazz CDs to cigarette cards, provided that enough prospects can be identified.

Once you've found a segment (or niche in the market) then demand tends to be governed by expertise, product knowledge and availability rather than low price. Committed buyers will return and more importantly pass recommendations. Your task then is to find more products or expand the service into that widening customer base and to develop a loyal following.

KEEPING THE CUSTOMER HAPPY

Other than competing on price – which is not normally the road to riches – you must find a niche in the market where others are falling down or not meeting demand. As the world shrinks and the Internet becomes more common, the consumer is getting more sophisticated and demands better service and a wider range of products. Take travel agents. Every high street has offices of the national chains but you will soon discover that most are owned by the tour operators who are pushing their own wares. There is a restricted choice. The market is getting more sophisticated with a slackening of demand for crowded package resorts and a growing interest in more exotic places and for independent travel.

This demand is met by small independent operators who cannot get a toe in the high street and have to sell 'off the page' in the Sunday papers. There must be a niche for the enterprising independent travel agent who can sell face to face.

The book trade is dominated by Waterstones, W H Smith, Dillons etc but there is scope for a specialist who stocks in depth. One bookshop in London stocks *nothing* but computer books – and does very well. People will travel a long way, or order by post, knowing that there is a very good chance that their demand will be stocked. It is the *service*, not the price, that is paramount. Richer Sounds, the hi-fi chain, has been built up entirely by obsessive attention to service to where it is now in the *Guinness Book of*

Records as the shop with the highest turnover per square foot in the world. They sell all branded goods that are obtainable at many other places, but they have succeeded by understanding the customer and by valuing their staff.

Big firms are bureaucratic and slow to change. Small firms should be quicker on their feet and better able to spot trends and fashion. Innovation should be your watchword. New ideas, new product lines, new offers and gimmicks keep your customers interested and alert. It stops *you* getting bored or stale. The firm that stands still declines. Not all of your ideas will work, but try a sample run and change things in stages, taking stock at each step. Monitor enquiries and sales and learn as you go along. New ideas come from reading your trade or technical press (every sector has at least one publication) and visiting your trade show at the NEC or in London. Those publications not found on the bookstall can be tracked down by reference to *BRAD* (British Rate and Data) or *Willings Press Guide* (both can be found in a reference library). Details of forthcoming exhibitions (public as well as trade) can be found in *Exhibition Bulletin*, a monthly periodical in your local library. New ideas are often launched at these venues to test reaction, and because hiring space is so expensive the top people are there to button-hole. Make use of the opportunity.

NEEDS AND BENEFITS

Nobody buys anything without having a need, and all your marketing should be directed at isolating what the consumer needs and matching that with the benefits of ownership. For example, you could argue that drill salesmen are not selling bits but holes, Kodak not films but memories. Computer people have a habit of describing features and not the benefits. '64Mb of superfast RAM plus 512k pipeline cache' instead of 'a big memory avoids computer crashes'. All your promotional material should be written from the point-of-view of the user not the seller. Try and place yourself in the mind of the target audience.

ADVERTISING

Most businesses will have to advertise but the medium selected will of course depend on the market you are trying to attract. It is very easy to spend a lot of money with little reward so bear in mind that:

- [ ] the key is to identify your target audience;
- [ ] you need to decide how to reach most of them at the lowest cost.

Don't be misled by large circulation or readership. Wastage may be enormous and more expensive than running a small ad in a precisely targeted magazine under the right heading. The main-stream opportunities to advertise include:

- [ ] local papers, local radio – freesheets tend to be thrown away quicker than papers that are paid for;
- [ ] your own vehicles and premises signs – make the most of your location;
- [ ] handbills, leaflets, brochures;
- [ ] specialist magazines from *Autocar* to *Exchange & Mart*;
- [ ] *Yellow Pages*, directories and year books;
- [ ] point of sales stickers, hangers, calendars, diaries.

Most printed papers and magazines work off what is called a rate card that sets out the standard sizes and advertising rates in mono and colour. The price will vary enormously. All newspapers offer classified small ads but some magazines only offer more expensive display adverts. Display ads can often be bought at knock down rates at the last minute, so always haggle. Within the rate card will be extravagant claims over readership (not to be confused with circulation – always far less – and is invariably ABC audited). Readership profiles on age, sex, and occupation will be listed but common sense and your own knowledge of the market should be observed.

The local press will be important to you as many areas enjoy very high readership. Don't overlook the small ads, as many people seem to read the classifieds from cover to cover. Be aware that there are limitations on what will reproduce: the paper used is generally poor, so don't expect fine type or pictures to print very well.

Design

You can either leave the design of the advert to the magazine or newspaper, though they will still want a rough, or produce it all yourself. With most papers containing hundreds of adverts your first task is to grab attention. This can be done by a headline or illustration. Put this at the top – not your name. An advert is a selling medium, so make sure you promise a benefit, and answer the selfish but realistic question, 'What's in it for me?'. You then expand on the headline in the text, not forgetting the essentials like price, ordering mechanism, shop hours if appropriate, guarantees and any other persuasive arguments, as long as space permits. Reversed type (white on black) is all right for large simple typefaces, but often becomes illegible when used for text. Make it difficult for the reader and they won't bother, so stick to simple messages with instant appeal which concentrate on why your reader should buy your product or service. An equally hard task for any advert is to promote action. You want readers to act – not discard the paper.

Be different

New firms with small promotional budgets need to get their money back. Try not to design 'me-too' advertising but differentiate the message and appeal. Make your ads distinctive and arresting so they are remembered and acted upon. That may mean becoming a little quirky but why not buck the trend for boring uninformative ads? You can achieve this by using unexpected items in your ad ('Double Glazing found in 16th Century Cottages' – Everest), bold headlines ('Smell the East with Small Party Travel'), tempting headlines ('Remember when fuel was just £1.59 a gallon? It still is' – Jet LPG).

Budget your advertising as part of your overall marketing strategy. Costing will be very important. However, bear in mind that whether you use an agency or place advertisements yourself, you get a reduction in price for block booking a number of advertisements. Monitor the level of response to your advertisements, noting not only how many respond but how many actually purchase. *Yellow Pages* (YP) is probably the most widely used advertising medium amongst small firms, but you need to adopt some common sense. In my experience, _YP_ adverts work for those purchases where the buyer does not have a regular supplier. We are all creatures of habit and tend to stick to those we know. The real problem arises for those congested areas like kitchen installation, double glazing and builders. How is your small budget ad going to stand out amongst the whole page extravagance of national purveyors? There is little point in shouting 'We're the best' or 'We're the cheapest'. You have to differentiate your offering by your _locality_ (all things being equal, people tend to travel to their nearest supplier), your stock range, specialised knowledge or some attribute (USP: Unique Selling Proposition) that only you can claim.

PUBLIC RELATIONS

PR is the least used marketing tool of small firms, yet the principles and methods are relatively easy to grasp. While PR has many facets – charity work, open days, sponsorship, newsletters, amongst many others – it is publicity direct to the media that should be your main thrust. With a little guidance most publicity can be undertaken on a local level by any competent businessman. It means studying the papers and specialist journals that fit your target segment and picking out what makes news. What is commonplace to you, because you do it every week, may be of newsworthy interest to some readers and, more importantly, the editor. Every firm tries to get in the national papers and mass circulation magazines, so unless you have some very riveting story, don't bother.

It is trite but has been proven many times that you stand more chance of getting in the papers if you can tie it to animals, babies, royalty, crime, local personalities and, unfortunately, sex. Above all it must be topical.

Recently a small traditional basket making firm in Somerset made a dog basket for the Queen's corgis. They make hundreds of baskets every year, so where was the news? Well the story made most of the national papers, including page 3 of _The Sun_, and Radio Montreal did a live broadcast in French. When you analyse what was the actual news, most businessmen's view of the press is confirmed.

When writing a press release it is worth bearing in mind the following points:

- [ ] print the words 'press release' at the top of the sheet;
- [ ] use a short headline to identify the story;
- [ ] use wide margins for printer's corrections;
- [ ] have a news slant to the press release rather than an advert for your business;
- [ ] customise it for different media;
- [ ] keep the text brief with the main point presented in the first sentence or two;
- [ ] keep it to one or two A4 pages using double line spacing;
- [ ] remember to include your contact details;
- [ ] photos that are included must be of a professional standard;
- [ ] include local TV and radio stations.

An effective public relations campaign can do your firm a lot of good, but don't expect instant results. PR should be treated as a long-term strategy to raise the profile and image of your business. Journalists in your chosen sector should be cultivated and regularly fed with interesting stories so that eventually, they will come to you for news.

DIRECT MAIL

Direct mail has trebled in volume over the last ten years, but it is no easy task to avoid the label 'junk mail' and generate a profitable response.

Successful direct mail relies on four factors:

1. the quality of the mailing list: the target fit and accuracy;
2. the message: perceived benefits and relevance to the reader;
3. overall costs of the promotion;
4. response rate.

You should devote most time, thought and money to compiling the list, not designing the sales message. Many firms only think of the target audience at the last moment. You can start to collect your own circulation list from market research, existing clients and advertising responses; or, if you wish to go about it more quickly, you can rent or buy a compiled list from a list broker. The Institute of Direct Marketing, 1 Park Road, Teddington, Middlesex TW11 0AR, tel 0181-977 5705, will send you a list of brokers. List brokers will sell – or more likely rent – you lists of everything from wealthy people in Mayfair to buyers of stretch covers. The cost will vary from £95 per thousand names to perhaps £250 per thousand depending on the quality and exclusivity of the list. Most have a minimum charge of around £300. Rental lists are for one time use only and will have concealed 'sleepers' of friends or employees to pick up unauthorised successive mailings.

Careful selection of your list is very important as it directly affects your response rate. The national average for direct mail is usually considered to be two per cent, but there can be wild fluctuations on this, including nil. The great advantage of direct mail over other forms of promotion is that you can try and test different offers, and learn the results very quickly, certainly within a week. It is statistically irrelevant to mail less than a thousand, but providing the remainder of your mailing list matches the test roll, then you can proceed on the results with greater confidence.

It is important to address the letter to the specifier, the decision maker, ideally by name or at least by job title if you are mailing to the trade. Consumer mailings, which tend to be far less rewarding for the small firm, should never be addressed to 'The Occupier'.

Below are seven further points to bear in mind:

1. You have no more than two seconds from starting the letter to convince the reader to continue, otherwise it will be junked. Your first headline and sentence are crucial.
2. Avoid putting too much text down, as you want to keep the reader's attention. You are not writing a story, you are selling your product.
3. You need to send at least four items. The sales letter, brochure, order form and reply envelope. If feasible, samples are

helpful. Faxback forms are probably more likely to produce a response from business than a reply paid envelope.

4. Try to send each mailing in a white envelope rather than a brown one. The presentation has a better appearance although it is more expensive. Remember, the envelope can also be used as part of the overall campaign.

5. Make sure that your mailer makes it easy for potential clients to reply. Special offers and free samples can be used.

6. Depending on the volume and on whether you can afford the cost, try to use at least two-colour printing for the brochure.

7. Don't mail an unproven product. The returns could cripple you. Surprisingly fragile products can be posted, but the costs of packaging could kill the profit. Test, test, test.

When you receive your replies, assess your response rate and monitor the sales. If necessary, the copy can then be amended to attract other clients on subsequent mail shots; make sure each different mailer is coded so that monitoring is easy and effective.

Upon receipt of replies, do ensure that each one is dealt with swiftly and professionally by either your sales team or by the relevant customer service person. If further details are required then these must be sent out promptly. There is no point in initiating a response if your service is slow off the mark or non-existent.

THE INTERNET

The Internet has been described as the world's biggest library without a catalogue or index. Therein lies the problem, for a vast amount of information would be available if only you could access it. Impressive figures are quoted for US sales via the Net but the promise has yet to be fulfilled for most UK advertisers looking for real income. So while experience is patchy and authenticated figures elusive the following may be helpful:

☐ people have to be aware of the Web site so quote the address in all your promotional material;

☐ make best use of the medium by making it interactive. Ask questions, filter enquirers so that you can better target your response and encourage feedback;

☐ link with other sites and companies;

☐ update regularly and don't allow it to become stale;

☐ include newsy items and hints and tips;

☐ don't get carried away with technology: not every visitor will have the latest or fastest gizmo.

The greatest success seems to lie with technology and scientific based products (invariably computers, defence related, higher educational, medical instruments and mechanical components of all sorts). The used car trade is doing well as in-stock cars can be updated daily. Specialist books are selling well. Net users are invariably and overwhelmingly masculine. A few small firms have reported success in selling to the States – even finding agents – where Net users outnumber us by 10 to 1. See Chapter 12 for further information.

SHOWS AND EXHIBITIONS

Running a stand can be an effective way of widening your market. Apart from rural craft and agricultural shows there are some 3000 trade and other significant public exhibitions run each year at venues as expensive as the NEC at Birmingham to an off-season hotel in Torquay. There are shows to cater for everyone's interests, from *Hotelympia* (now at Earls Court) to the Royal Show at Stoneleigh (300,000 visitors). If you have designed a new dog collar, head for *Petindex* at Harrogate, a better tractor then go to Smithfield and so on; these shows are worth attending. To find major shows look in *Exhibition Bulletin* (updated every month), or for smaller rural shows, *The Showman's Directory* (copies probably in your reference library).

Whatever your budget, get hold of last year's show catalogue and gauge from the exhibitors if it is the right arena for you. General shows are usually of less use than those more specific. If you can't afford to rent an entire stand, try contacting another exhibitor to share the costs and manning by offering a commission on leads generated. Shows are also good places to visit to meet key players and keep up to date on the competition.

Multi-level marketing

Once outlawed as pyramid selling, network marketing or multi-level marketing has returned under more ethical rules. There is still the need to be wary about venturing into such a field with its promises of easy riches for little effort. It works well in the States, but is still viewed with some scepticism over here. Do your own sums and work out if the balance of profit is too heavily weighted in favour of those at the top, rewarding the humble foot sloggers with very little margin.

SALES

Your sales force is your front line and it is your salesmen's skill that ensures a healthy turnover of contracts. Although this is stating the obvious, no matter how many administrative systems or accounting procedures you have, your company could not exist without sales. Selling is a skill, it is a combination of job commitment, product knowledge and the ability to put across the point which tells the client what he wants to hear so that he buys the product or service on offer. The closing of the sale is as necessary as initiating the contract. This holds true for both on-the-road sales personnel and for telephone sales (the latter is more cost-effective and can be used with great benefit as a back-up or customer supply service).

Many businessmen find it difficult to sell and this comes across to the customer. If you are a sole trader or in a small partnership or company, you will have to train yourself to go out and sell your product – remembering that selling is a two-way communication. Remember that the national average for selling situations is supposed to be one successful call to seven rejections, so your hardest task is probably going to be maintaining your own morale and enthusiasm. Good salesmen enjoy meeting people and are interested in what makes them tick. Much of selling is trying to understand that simple psychology of the individual buyer.

Meet the buyer

While there will always be 'born salesmen' many can master enough of the rudiments to earn a living. You must first grasp that people buy people: in other words you have to sell yourself first, the product later. Image, personality and belief in oneself are vital, for no-one buys from bored and disinterested salesmen. Appointments should be made where possible. You need to identify the correct decision maker and get past the receptionist whose job may be to deflect all salesmen. Providing you adopt an honest, straightforward approach and avoid time wasting irrelevance, you should be able to make appointments in most cases. Be firm and authoritative, yet polite. Record all names, as it flatters people's egos to use the name next time. It sometimes helps to offer alternatives: 'I am in your area next Wednesday and Thursday. Which is more convenient?' The choice then is not whether the buyer will see you or not but which day is the more suitable.

Good salesmen are good listeners but not good talkers. Selling is a two way conversation – the trick is to show interest in the buyer's problems and provide the attractive solution. Keep the initial pleasantries to a minimum and then:

☐ always ask open questions that cannot be answered by just saying 'yes' or 'no';
☐ know your product and have correct prices and delivery dates to hand;
☐ look for buying indicators: questions that mean 'I'd like some of those.' If the buyer asks 'Do you do them in red?' it really means sell me some;
☐ take samples where possible and encourage the prospect to handle or try them on. Involve all the senses. If the product needs demonstrating make sure it works properly beforehand;
☐ ask for an order and probe the objection.

Handling objections

Inevitably there will be objections: too dear, existing supplier, budget already allocated, wrong time of the year, don't deal with new (or small) suppliers, not enough discount or margin, no brand awareness or national advertising – and doubtless many more. Don't be discouraged and don't expect to walk out with an order every time. First visits are fishing expeditions to find out if the prospect has any need for your product range, what price and quantity tend to be bought, and to learn of any seasonality in purchasing. The first sale should be in the nature of a sample order: 'try us out, compare our service with your existing supplier, keeps him on his toes.' Once a relationship and trust has developed between you, real selling is more likely to take place. Buyers, be they in industry or in the home, tend to stick with suppliers they trust and it takes time to break down those prejudices. As a race we tend not be adventurous and risk our – or the boss's – money.

Closing the sale

Closing the sale means obtaining an order and this is where the better salesman scores. Answers to objections can often be turned into a closing question.

- ☐ 'I need them by next week.' 'If I can rush them through how many would you like?'
- ☐ 'I've spent my budget for this year.' 'Tell me when your new year starts.'
- ☐ 'I've no room to hold stock.' 'Fine, we'll make weekly deliveries instead of monthly.'
- ☐ 'I need a bigger margin.' 'We'll meet your price if you order 10% more.'

Never be afraid of simply asking for an order. The buyer is then forced to come to a decision, and often an objection, which may lead to an opening if you listen and react. Often the buyer will have to consult with others, perhaps a committee, and further appointments will have to be made. Keep up the momentum by writing a reminder letter or phoning after a sensible period.

It sometimes helps to leave a sample behind so that the buyer's colleagues can handle the product, and this also provides a further opportunity to call back. And before you leave, ask for someone else, perhaps within his organization, that you can see: 'By the way is there anyone I might usefully see?'

Some golden rules

☐ Identify your market segment and look for the gaps.
☐ Study trends, decide where there is growth and profit.
☐ Think about what the customer needs and talk about benefits.
☐ Always answer the question 'What's in it for me?'
☐ Make your product different and your ads distinctive.
☐ Find other goodies to sell into your growing customer base.
☐ Cosset the customer and always keep your promises.

Presentations

A professional image must be presented at all times.

Here are a few further 'golden rules' to bear in mind when presenting to customers or speaking to them on the telephone:

☐ never promise what you cannot deliver;
☐ never let your customer see that you have a problem;
☐ never be too pushy or aggressive as this can lose a sale;
☐ never criticise your competitors – the attitude to take is 'they are good, but we are better', or simply do not mention them;
☐ never criticise your colleagues or the business or its product(s);
☐ never argue with the customer – turn the point around by asking questions.

The main area in which sales are lost in a presentation is in the closing of the sale. Some people are frightened to ask for a commitment and avoid the closing question. Be positive, ask the customer: 'When shall we deliver?' 'Do we agree that ...?' 'Do I have your approval on ...?' 'Do you want it if we can get it?' 'How many would you like?' It is a waste of time to make a presentation, get the customer interested and then back away from asking for a commitment at the last moment. The customer will not mind being asked.

MOTIVATING SALESPEOPLE

Salespeople need management, motivation and control; recognition of a job well done develops a sense of achievement. It is relatively easy to see when a salesman is not working well but it is more difficult to find out why. Be sympathetic and try to find out the reasons for the lack of or decrease in sales performance. It is a good idea to have a commission rate system based on performance but at the same time it should be linked to security by the provision of a basic salary. An appreciative thank you is often worth nearly as much as a bonus. Selling is a lonely, often dispiriting, and misunderstood job, so always give your sales force support and encouragement. It helps to learn what motivates them: we are all individuals.

Sales are the life-blood of a business: without the selling of your product, you would not be in business at all.

Checklist: Marketing

☐ Have you a marketing plan?
☐ Have you costed your publicity effort?
☐ What should your publicity achieve?
☐ Will you provide transport?
☐ What packaging and delivery policy will you have?
☐ Have you prepared your pricing policy to meet the market opportunity?
☐ Will you avoid undercutting your experienced and established competitors' prices?
☐ Are your quality, service and price strategies adequate?
☐ Is there any unique feature about your offer?
☐ Are you better, cheaper, quicker, or all of these, than your experienced competitors?
☐ Will you do your own selling?
☐ Will you offer sales people commission (on profit or turnover?)
☐ What will your selling effort cost?
☐ What else should be considered in your case?

Source: *DfEE, Small Firms Section, Running your Own Business*

---

6 | Control and Financial Management

January 1999 saw the birth of the Euro – a single currency for all 'Euroland' with nearly 300 million people and a 20 per cent share of world GDP. Centrally set interest rates started in 1999 at 6 per cent which compares with 6 per cent in the UK and taken together with the relatively high value of sterling would seem to put UK businesses at some disadvantage.

Problems in emerging market countries in Asia and South America have added to the domestic uncertainty of where the UK economy is heading. Manufacturing and retail sectors are both struggling as evidenced by warnings of sales and profit shortfalls. Even large companies like Marks and Spencer have not proved to be immune to the downturn.

The economic climate is difficult for anyone setting up in a new business and the risk of failure is very high. But if you do set out on your own, or seize an opportunity for growth and development of an existing business, then effective control is vital if you are to survive and succeed. Yet very often we find that it is exactly this ingredient which is missing. The businessman gets on with what he considers the real work – and neglects the controls and forward planning – and his business suffers accordingly.

PLANNING

One factor which affects small and large businesses alike is the rate of change. During the last few years we have seen an accelerating rate of change: products are on sale today, some of them by using new technology, that were not even thought of ten or even five years ago. In this climate, planning – especially financial planning – is of the utmost importance. The well-managed company needs to be constantly alert to change. The prime questions to ask yourself are:

- [ ] Where are we now?
- [ ] Where do we want to go?
- [ ] What resources (financial and manpower) do we have?
- [ ] What is our performance like?
- [ ] What are our objectives?
- [ ] How are we going to reach them?
- [ ] What is holding us back?
- [ ] What tactics do we use?
- [ ] What is the competition?

Then, as managers, we have to start to make it happen.

FIXING YOUR OBJECTIVES

Let us start at the beginning. Where do we want to go? Write your objectives down. If you do not know where you want to go, your chances of arriving are not good.

Identifying the constraints

The next step is to ask: 'What constraints are holding us back?' Typically the answers fall into three main areas: finance, management and markets.

Finance

The worst time to go to your bank and ask to borrow money is when you are in desperate need of it; when this happens it is often the result of poor financial control. Statistics show that a high proportion of companies go bust within the first four years. Most insolvencies can be avoided if the management directs proper attention to cash-flow problems. A major deficiency in small businesses is often a lack of 'information' about the cash requirements. But information concerning what? The answer is: cash flow and profitability.

Financial control involves dealing effectively with each of the individual steps in the cycle:

☐ having the necessary information to facilitate day-to-day management of the assets and liabilities of the business, particularly the debtors and creditors;

☐ having the right information to plan the overall cash needs of the business and to evaluate the worth of future projects and alternative proposals;

☐ having the information needed for measuring actual results and comparing them with the plan;

☐ having advance information to enable the business to do a proper job of tax planning.

Each business has different financial pressure points, ranging from effective debtor control to seasonal peaks and sudden large payments. It is the gathering of such information that is an important ingredient in solving potential financial problems.

It is vital to make sure that either you have sufficient cash reserves, or you are able to look ahead to when you may need the money. If you can make a good case for it and show that you have a profitable idea, often it is not that difficult to raise the money (in which case, it was not really a financial constraint in the first place). Alternatively, when you work the proposal out carefully, it may not look such a good idea after all and you will be unable to raise the money – but in that case it was only because the business plan was faulty in the first place.

Management

Starting off in a small business you may not be lucky enough to have any managerial assistance, in which case you have to become a 'jack of all trades'. This situation may not last, however, and once you start to expand, increasing your turnover and the size of your company or business, you need to consider the extra managerial layer needed – middle management. The first type of management expertise you need may be in the financial and sales/marketing areas. You could find that some of your employees 'in the back room' have hidden talents which could be useful to you. But in any case this is the time when you have to be very careful that your control structure and overheads are in line with your activities.

As your business grows and your middle management expertise needs to be 'bought in', make sure first of all that it cannot be found in existing employees. Consultants can be expensive and selecting those suitable to your business's needs is time-consuming. Before employing a consultant seek recommendations first. Always select a reputable firm and one which has had previous working experience in your field of business. Enquire as to the size of company the firm normally works for. Above all, consider whether you can afford their fees. To some extent these points apply to any external professionals you engage, such as your accountant or solicitor.

As each department is formed, you must be careful that guidelines are laid down so that the workload and personnel supervision are clearly defined. This is often a weak point in medium-sized companies. As your company expands further and you find that you are no longer able to oversee all the departments, the time has come to appoint a general manager.

Arthur C Clarke, the science fiction writer, sums it up very nicely: 'The company which concentrates on the present may have no future; in business as in everyday life, wisdom lies in striking a balance between the needs of today and those of tomorrow. It is true that the farmer whose house is on fire must stop the sowing to put out the fire, but he will lose much more than his house if he doesn't prepare for next year's crop.'

Markets

Financial planning is not just looking inwards – it must look outwards as well. One of the hardest things for a small business to do is to keep an eye on what is going on outside. It is very important that you do not lose sight of what is happening around you. All products go through a traditional cycle: introduction, growth, maturity, saturation, decline and obsolescence. Sometimes it takes generations, sometimes it takes two or three months. Skateboards are a good example. They were introduced in early 1980 and grew to maturity by early autumn but the fad was virtually over by December. Lots of people made a lot of money on skateboards but most of them lost it again at the end of the cycle because they did not get out quickly enough. This all boils down to 'timing'. In later years, skateboards re-emerged with more sophisticated designs that allowed greater manoeuvrability and enhanced performance, so starting a new product cycle that was to prove more lasting if not as frenetic.

It is often recommended that you keep an 'Ideas' file in which you and your employees can put down any feasible suggestions. Look at the prevailing market influences and consider whether or not you can afford to produce (in both monetary and physical terms) a new product. It may be too late once your competitors have introduced a new product to decide whether or not you should attempt to match it. Once you have borne all these considerations in mind, however, you will be wise to plan to move with the market force.

Let us consider the case of Brut, the range of men's toiletries, which was introduced many years ago as a very high-class product. It went through the inevitable cycle, and when it began to decline the company made it available through outlets like Boots, Woolworths and so on. In this way they gave new life to the product by widening the market. When sales began to drop off again, they introduced not just aftershave but also body lotion and talc, as well as all toiletries they already sold under a different brandname. Once more they widened the product range and the market, and Brut took off again. Then when it began to decline once more they brought in Henry Cooper with a big advertising campaign to promote their products. The big companies can afford to do that – they have the resources – but as a smaller company you will not be able to take such an aggressive market line, and so you will have to be prepared to move with the market.

This is where market research helps. If you cannot afford to hire the services of a specialist firm, compile a simple questionnaire and ask your sales force to circulate it. The information gained from it can then be analysed, and will help in making overall decisions about your product. Get to know your market-

Managing the Biggest Risks

Setting up and running a business inevitably involves some risk. For a start, business loans are often secured on private property, and a lifetime of savings may be invested in the venture. Lack of credit facilities in the early days can place heavy demands on cash flow, and in the midst of an ever evolving market place and intense competition, new products need to become established as quickly as possible if a fledgling business is going to survive. Add to this the potential risks to the health and welfare of the entrepreneur and suddenly the odds begin to look formidable.

And yet every year countless entrepreneurs launch successful new businesses despite the risks. So what is the secret to taking on the odds, dealing with the stress, and achieving the ambition?

Firstly, most successful entrepreneurs probably have a clear vision of what they want and expect to achieve from their proposed business venture. This vision will reach way beyond the shorter term stresses and risks mentioned above, but that does not mean that the risks are simply ignored, far from it!

Secondly, with the vision of the future as the starting point, successful business people will develop a concise plan, probably in writing, of how they will move forward to achieve the goals they have set. It is this planning process which, if done properly, will consider all the risks and threats faced by the venture and determine how best to deal with them. Careful planning is very often the key ingredient of successful businesses, large and small.

But risk comes in various forms. Some are obvious but difficult to plan for in advance, such as a volatile market or the emergence of a new competitor's product. Some are equally as obvious but can be eliminated easily, like the chances of the premises being destroyed by fire. But there is a third kind of risk which is potentially the most dangerous of all because, firstly, the consequences could be as devastating as a fire, but secondly, it is not an obvious risk to some new entrepreneurs so no plans are made to manage it (even though it is often quite straight forward to eliminate it).

This third kind of risk is the danger that one of the key people involved in driving the business forward becomes unavailable to carry out their crucial duties. This may be as a result of death or a serious illness, or in later years it may be that they simply want to retire! But the problem faced by an ill-prepared business when it loses a partner, director, or other key person in this way, is that the organisation gets hit from all sides.

Firstly there is the loss of the unique contribution of the person, (suppose they had all the technical expertise, or maybe they were responsible for 80% of sales, or they could have been the master craftsman). Secondly, the business will suddenly have to find the cash to buy out the ex-partner or director's share at a time when profits are likely to be hard hit due to his departure. And thirdly, the loss of such a key member of the team can damage confidence with the business' bankers, making lending very difficult or impossible at a time when cash (and lots of it) may be crucial to survival.

It is very important that all business people are fully aware of the risk posed by losing a key player in their organisation. Financial planning of this sort should be an integral part of the business plan. After all, there is a 1 in 6 chance that a male aged 30 will suffer a heart attack before reaching age 65 (Source: ERC Frankona). It is far too big a risk to ignore.

Help is at hand. For instance, CGU, one of the UK's largest insurers with outlets world wide and £110 bn funds, has a team of dedicated Corporate Financial Consultants whose purpose is to assist business people to plan for both the unexpected (such as early loss of a partner) and the inevitable (retirement or death).

They can show, clearly and simply, how CGU's range of Partnership and Director schemes can be used to protect profits against the death or incapacity of the business owners. These schemes can ensure that sufficient cash is available to take care of the departing member or his family, as well as helping to make sure the business can continue to function effectively through the period of disruption.

Additionally, these Consultants can show how careful pension planning will maximise retirement benefits whilst minimising the tax bill, and also how the pension fund may be used by the business in future to provide cash in a crisis or to fund expansion plans.

You can make an appointment to speak with one of CGU's Corporate Financial Consultants by calling 0500 103 103 and quoting reference 1085. There is no fee and no obligation to act on any recommendations made, and all consultations are strictly confidential.

Managing a business means managing the risks. Make sure you are covered!

For your security, your call with CGU may be recorded and/ or monitored. Any financial advice given will relate only to the products of CGU.

CGU Life Assurance Limited Registered in England No. 226742, 2 Rougier Street York YO90 1UU

Telephone: 0500 103 103 Quote Ref: 1085

Regulated by the Personal Investment Authority

Which of the following will play the biggest part in making your new business a success?

- The size and location of the premises
- The quality and make of machinery or other equipment
- The age and number of vehicles used
- The skill and efforts of the partners/directors

Now, which of these were you planning to insure?

At CGU we know it is the quality and effectiveness of people, not plant or equipment, that makes a business successful. Our professional Corporate Financial Consultants give practical advice on our competitive range of:

- Partnership and Director protection packages
- Sickness Schemes
- Pension Arrangements

To make a no obligation appointment call us FREE on

0500 103103

and quote reference 1085.

Business is a risky venture. Don't take more risk than you need to.

Any financial advice given will relate only to the products of CGU. For your security, your call with CGU may be recorded and/or monitored.

CGU Life Assurance Limited
Registered in England No. 226742
2 Rougier Street York YO90 1UU
Regulated by the Personal Investment Authority

place and which products it can take; it is no use producing a walking, talking, tail-wagging toy if there are others like it on the market, or if potential buyers will not accept it.

TYPES OF CONTROL

The structure of the business

The organisation of the business itself is a control. The fact that there is an organisation with directors and divisional managers, with even the simplest of administrative/financial/sales/production functions, demonstrates this. The business is structured in a pyramid fashion. When applied to the company's organisation this means a formal workload/personnel ratio. When a company becomes either too top heavy (with too many senior managers or middle managers) or the opposite, where there are not enough senior/middle managers, it is harmful for business and should be avoided at all costs.

Job functions

Segregation of functions is a control much loved by accountants. The fact that, in a business, people will have to do different things to the same document is a form of control. In a typical situation one person in a department will place an order, but another person in a different department will pay the invoice relating to that order. If fraud is to take place it will require collusion between at least two parties. So too in the preparation of the payroll, segregation of duty helps to prevent loss to the business.

Physical controls

Physical controls include the lock on the petty cash box, the fence round the factory, the list of who uses the company cars and how many miles they have done, who has the authority to order what, etc.

_____

MANAGEMENT ACCOUNTS FOR THE MONTH ENDED:

| | This month | | Cumulative year to date | | |
| | Actual | Budget | Actual | Budget | Variance |

ANY COMPANY LTD
Last year

Month   Year to date
£000 % of sales   £000 % of sales

	£000	% of sales	£000	% of sales	£000	% of sales	£000	% of sales	£000	% of budget
SALES		100		100		100		100		
Cost of sales										
GROSS PROFIT										
Commission payable										
Carriage and packing										
Bad debts provision										
Rent and rates										
Light, heat and power										
Insurance										
Repairs and renewals										
Directors' remuneration										
Other employment costs										
Travelling and motor expenses										
Printing, stationery and advertising										
Telephone and postage										
General expenses										
Audit and other professional fees										
Hire and leasing costs										
Depreciation										
Bank charges and interest										
Other items (service charge receivable)										
TOTAL OVERHEADS										
NET PROFIT (LOSS) BEFORE TAX										

Figure 6.1: *Monthly management account report*

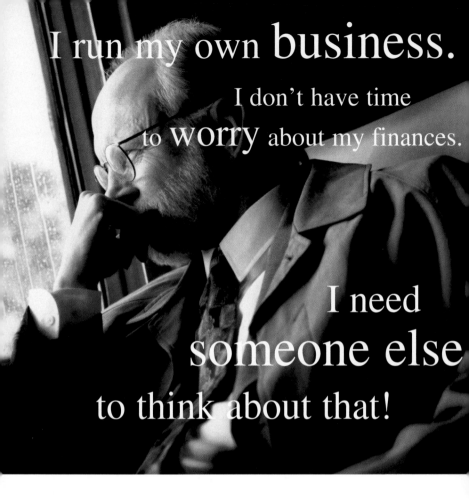

I run my own business.

I don't have time to worry about my finances.

I need someone else to think about that!

You run your own business because you value your independence. And independence means protecting your business. Especially its key asset – you!

At Lincoln, it's our job to make protecting you, your family, your business clear and understandable. You talk, we listen. Only then will we offer our advice. In a world that's complex enough, you'll be glad to know that it'll be simplicity itself!

Call Lincoln free on **0800 783 0222**. and we'll arrange for you to talk to one of our financial consultants.

Clear solutions in a complex world

Lincoln
Member of Lincoln Financial Group

GROW WITH US

Like a new English rose, the BB*f*S Holloway Plan has been carefully cultivated to offer you a refreshingly different approach to both ill-health income protection and saving for retirement.

The big difference is that your contributions combine to not only guarantee an income during sickness, but also produce a tax free* lump sum when you reach age 60.

Such a simple approach has been providing financial security for generations of independent business people. Today, our members include men and women from all walks of life and the basic Plan has been extended with many extra refinements. You can even use it to make arrangements for a non-working spouse or a new-born child.

At BB*f*S you will find a reassuringly cultured approach to doing business.

FREEPHONE 0800 975 6565

BB*f*S

BRITISH BENEFITS *friendly* SOCIETY LIMITED

No.1 TREVOR STREET, BEDFORD, MK40 2AB.
FACSIMILE: 01234 327879

Authorisation

Authorisation means that everything has to be approved by somebody. The most common example is that cheques can only be signed if they are authorised by a senior manager in charge of that section. If there are two directors then a system should be arranged whereby two signatures are needed. Orders too have to be signed by someone in authority to be valid.

Finance

Accounting controls include such things as someone going through invoices to check that they are added up correctly and relate to goods and services actually received. Other examples are ensuring that ledgers are balanced, that bank statements are reconciled, that management accounts balance and that in annual accounts the balance sheet adds up. All outgoings and incomings should ideally be analysed and accounting controls established for prompt invoicing, stock control and credit control. The production of a budgeted profit and loss account will enable a comparison with the actual results to identify variations, as shown in Figure 6.1 (on page 86). It will also provide the major part of the information required to enable you to produce a cash-flow forecast which will give you and your bank manager a forewarning of any future cash problems (see Chapter 7).

PERSONNEL CONTROLS

Ensure that you employ people fit for the job, that they have had appropriate training, that they know what to do and that they are reliable.

Management

Supervision of members of staff is a form of control. If you have an invoicing section, there could be a need for a supervisor of that department, depending upon the size of your company

One **Business** is **Leading**

the profession of

Financial
Planning

HAMBRO FRASER SMITH

Innovative
financial planning
with
Traditional
private client
Values

- asset management
- tax mitigation
- business planning
- wealth creation

For

more

information call:

01707 672900

Hambro Fraser Smith Ltd. Regulated by the Personal Investment Authority. Offices in Pall Mall, London and Potters Bar, Hertfordshire. Associates throughout the UK.

HambroFraserSmith

The decision to work for yourself or run your own business brings with it a need for considerable self-discipline. This discipline is equally necessary for both the day-to-day working environment and long term financial security at both a business and personal level.

At the heart of this process is the development and implementation of a financial plan. The objective is to develop a vehicle for realising these personal and business aspirations which are, inevitably, inextricably linked for the business owner.

The first priority, though, is to develop the business plan. This covers a number of key areas such as your business focus, financial aspirations and budgets, a definition of target clients and the marketing mix designed to attract them to the business. In addition, the plan will set out the long term objectives for the business - for example the plans for realising capital on future sale.

Having decided upon these objectives, it is then prudent to consider associated financial matters.

There are a number of 'musts' which have to be addressed, including the chosen structure of the business (which could be as a sole trader, partnership or limited company), who owns the business and how it is to be financed by share or partnership capital and/ or loans. Accountancy and tax advice is necessary to assist with these decisions. Then, there are the legal matters to be attended to.

All business ventures need insurances of one type or another - such as professional indemnity, office insurances, public liability, motor vehicles etc. The precise levels and costs of cover must be identified and factored into the financing of the business. Some of these will be mandatory and some desirable.

It is also necessary to address other business risks, such as the impact that illness, injury or death will have on the business, its creditors and (most importantly) on personal and family circumstances. In undertaking such risk evaluation the following areas should be considered:-

- Shareholder/ partnership protection to ensure that the business is protected as a consequence of the death of a major participant. This insurance will mean that the survivors are not forced into unwelcome decisions created by the financial needs of the deceased's family.

- insurance for business loans or other business creditors

- critical illness insurance to cover the same liabilities but payable on the diagnosis of a serious illness such as a cancer, rather than on death (statistically the chances of suffering such a condition are three times greater than dying prior to retirement).

- permanent health insurance to ensure that income is protected in the event of prolonged absence from work due to illness or injury.

Great care is necessary when establishing such contingency insurance to establish the benefits and costs of the cover necessary and to consider the most tax efficient way of establishing the policies.

All business ventures are created with one major purpose in mind - to produce income and/or capital for those involved! Thus, it is only right that any financial plan (as a complement to the business plan itself) addresses the subject of wealth management.

This will include plans in how income should be extracted from the business in the most tax-efficient method - whether by salary, dividends or benefits. It is vitally important to strike the correct balance between providing income today and ensuring 'deferred remuneration' for retirement years - particularly as the government has placed greater responsibility on the individual to provide for their own security in retirement. This balance is equally important for any employees of the business.

Pension planning is one of the few remaining tax shelters with full tax relief on contributions paid into the pension scheme, tax advantaged growth in the fund and the opportunity to take benefits partly as tax free cash at the point of retirement. The interaction between private pension schemes with state benefits must also be taken into account, particularly as the structure is changing with the introduction of stakeholder pensions.

Many people starting up in business on their own account may also have pension rights from previous employment and consideration should be given to the merits of transferring these pension rights into a new scheme. Nowadays, self administered pension schemes are growing in popularity. They provide the facility to invest substantial sums for future retirement provision but also to access funds for reinvestment back into the business through loans, equity investment or purchase of the property from which the business operates.

One of the largest assets may be the value of the business, which many people view as their 'pension'. It is dangerous to rely on this principle alone and a combination of pre-funded retirement benefits (using approved and tax effective pension schemes) and the ability to realise capital from the sale of the business is a more responsible strategy. This is particularly so given the relatively high failure rate of new businesses often due to factors outside the control of their owners.

Whatever is decided, the overriding aim is to ensure that personal financial plans dovetail precisely with those of the business and that the activities of all advisers in supporting these goals and aspirations are fully integrated to meet the same identified objectives.

THE COMPANY

HambroFraserSmith has been formed from the combination of the UK's most progressive financial planning firm, Fraser Smith, with the backing of two of the City's leading financial figures - Rupert Hambro and Michael Hepher. The Hambro name has been synonymous with the provision of sound financial advice for over 150 years and has stood behind the development of some of the UK's most successful businesses; Michael Hepher has one of the most respected careers spanning the financial services and telecommunication industries.

With the growing complexity and sheer pace of modern financial life there is a significant demand for a truly holistic approach to managing total wealth - one that pulls together all the related elements of tax planning, asset management, business and family interests with the most creative deployment of income and capital. The service requires a fee based approach rather than the traditional commission driven system thereby enabling truly independent objectivity in the advice and implementation processes. HambroFraserSmith has been created to serve this need - combining both innovation and tradition.

**For further details,
please contact
HambroFraserSmith
Tel: 01707 672 900
Fax: 01707 672 901
Email: enquiries@hfs.co.uk**

*Regulated by the Personal Investment
Authority*

department and your turnover. If you have a shop, there will be one person who is in charge of the other assistant(s). The staff then know that if they have a problem there is a supervisor to approach, and that they do not have to go right to the very top, which might put them off.

Management has the task of ensuring that their employees' job specifications are in line with the company's objectives, and that all jobs are carried out satisfactorily. They, along with the other employees and the owners, should have the company's best interests at heart, from making sure that the products are selling at the right price and making the right profit, through receiving the cash and seeing that it does not go astray, to making sure that production is up to standard and looking after the welfare and status of the staff.

Cash management is a vital function in the overall management role, with the main aim being to generate more capital for the company, as well as to conserve the existing capital. There are a number of areas where this principle can be effectively applied, such as cost reduction, aggressive pricing, elimination of cash liquidation of excess assets, and cautious borrowing. Credit control (see Chapter 7), prompt invoicing, good banking arrangements and payments to suppliers are all areas which need attention.

The continuous monitoring of a business is an important management function. Monitoring may be broadly defined as the preparation and review of regular accounting information. It should include preparation of budgets, product costs and cash-flow forecasts, followed by the comparison of these projections with actual results on a regular basis.

The fact that your business is doing well does not mean that you can sit back; indeed, it can be said that you need to work even harder. Priorities need to be established concerning the day-to-day financial controls of the business and the regular reporting of results. Do not rely on the annual audit to determine the future of the company; by its nature, an audit deals in historical information and cannot normally be used to determine the strategy of the company.

The importance of regular financial information does not lie in its preparation; it is the intelligent review of the results and

Remorse *n.* Feeling or expression of sorrow; regret at one's actions.

Remortgage *n. & v.* A way of freeing money invested in a property in order to pay off debts etc.

Ask a bank for the latter, and you'll probably only get the former.

The response from building societies is likely to be equally definitive.

But at The Money Store, we specialise in offering remortgaging solutions to people who have run up sizeable debts. Our rates are very fair, and we work fast.

In fact, we could let you have the money you need within 7 days. Just imagine how you could be feeling this time next week, without the pressure of your current financial problems.

(Hint: see under 'relieved'.)

Lines are open 8am - 8pm Mon - Fri, 9am - 6pm Sat, and 10am - 6pm Sun.

0800 783 4448 THE MONEY STORE®

D O N ' T   T A K E   *N O*   F O R   A N   A N S W E R

Changing employment patterns have left more and more self-employed people and contract workers with problems in getting a mortgage from traditional lenders.

Lenders must protect themselves against taking on bad debt. But inflexible screening processes mean would-be borrowers who are perfectly able to repay the loan they want are still turned down – often through no fault of their own.

It may be, for example, that someone has recently set up their own business. The business could be doing perfectly well, but has simply not been running long enough to have the three years' of accounts which mainstream lenders will demand. Hence, the borrower is rejected.

Many people picked up a patchy credit record in the recession of the 1980s, perhaps missing one or two mortgages payments when times were particularly tight. Those payments may long since have been cleared, but still lead to a loan being refused.

Self-employed people with small businesses will inevitably have cash flow problems, often because larger customers are slow to pay their bills. Sometimes they will find their income is concentrated into a few very busy months of the year, making it hard to cope when this seasonal income falls away. Every year, 1.5 million County Court Judgements (CCJs) are issued. Again, these debts may have been cleared long since, but remain on your credit record for six years.

Even a small business which is established and successful today may still be dogged by a patchy credit record incurred during those very difficult first few years when the owner was fighting to get his business established.

Contract workers may find they move from a highly lucrative project into two or three months of unemployment. The chequered employment history this creates can also lead to future loan applications being turned down.

There is an answer

The fact is that the big lenders' systems are geared for mainstream business, and not for the growing number of self-employed applicants. Already there are 10 million self-employed, temporary or contract workers in the UK, with the number of self-employed predicted to increase by 18% in the next few years.

Self-employed people also tend to be older than other workers. There are more self-employed people aged over 40 than aged between 20 and 30. You may think this would be a point in their favour, as someone of 40 or more is likely to be a more responsible borrower than an applicant in their 20s. But, paradoxically, many big lenders reckon that being over 40 makes you not a better risk, but as worse one.

More and more of us will spend at least part of our lives working for ourselves. This can only mean that demand for loans from The Money Store will increase.

---

trends shown by that information which is essential to the successful running of the company. For example, the accounts may show that sales have fallen, but it is more important to understand why. There could be a simple answer, or the answer could rest with any one of a number of problems, from production problems to understaffing or defaulted deliveries. The information should be prepared on a regular basis. It is a good idea to prepare these accounts monthly, near the middle or the end of the month.

Controls prevent you getting lost. If things go wrong you can find out why, and do something about it quickly. If your business is going into loss or stops making a profit, then your controls (management accounts, cash figures and cash-flow forecast) will sound warning bells in time for you to take action. You will not be waiting until the end of the year or perhaps several months after that for your accountant to tell you that you made a loss of £10,000 last year. Your controls will have warned you that this is happening and you can do something about it.

Benchmarking

This term is applied to an ongoing control process to improve products, services and systems, by reference to the best practices in other companies. Financial and operational performance measures are compared with other organizations and working practices changed in those areas found to be weak.

The law

Controls also stop you breaking the law. If you pay people's wages without deducting tax or pay the wrong amount of VAT or are not observing the Health and Safety at Work Act – you are breaking the law. Controls in business prevent mistakes which, while they may be quite innocent, are nevertheless unlawful. Ignorance is no defence in the eyes of the law.

The essential thing for any business, large or small, is to have a strategy: to know where you are going and how you are

The start is just the beginning
A cautionary tale for the would-be self employed

At the last count, more than three million people in this country were self-employed*. Now representing around 13% of the UK's workforce, their numbers have increased by more than half since the beginning of the last decade.

But what is the attraction of being self-employed? For most people starting out, it's the thought of independence - making your own choices and reaping your own rewards. But even with luck on your side, success in your venture will only come with planning. It may be a cliché, but it's sadly still true to say that: 'We never plan to fail, we simply fail to plan'.

Planning doesn't only require an appreciation of the physical aspects of your future business. It's clearly important to identify basic necessities such as suppliers, premises, equipment needs and perhaps most importantly of all, customers. But as with all plans, it's also important to take steps to protect your business should the unforeseen happen.

Insurance is vital to any business plan. In addition to the sort of cover which most of us already have, to protect our car, office or the family home, there is also all manner of statutory requirements to think about. For example, if you're planning to employ someone, you'll need employer's liability insurance to cover them against accidents at work. And depending on the type of business you have, you may need public liability insurance or professional indemnity cover.

The need for protection doesn't stop there. Being self-employed puts you at the very cornerstone of your business. But despite this, even those who are well used to working for themselves fail to consider the implications of being unable to work. And yet this can have important repercussions for not only their business, but also themselves and their families.

According to a poll carried out by Continental Research, almost two thirds of the self-employed do not have any form of cover to provide a replacement income during periods of longer term illness. Yet going it alone means sacrificing the support of a sympathetic employer and accepting the prospect of only minimal support from the state. What's more, while being unable to work may prevent you from earning an income, it won't put a stop to the fixed costs which your business will continue to incur.

Remember being your own boss brings independence in all things – not only managing but also protecting the future of your business. So Lincoln recommends that you find an adviser who is able to suggest ways of protecting your most important asset – you.

Wayne Taylor,
Marketing Executive, Lincoln

Lincoln is a marketing group regulated by the Personal Investment Authority providing life assurance, pensions, unit trusts and ISAs.

National Statistical Office, Social Trends

If you run a business, have no need for overdraft facilities and generate less than 80 transactions each month - why are you still bank paying charges?

Investec Bank (UK) has developed a highly efficient postal banking service. This allows clients to conduct all of their banking at their own convenience, from the privacy of their office or home. At Investec Bank (UK) we are committed to providing our clients with a high standard of service and attach great importance to developing long term relationships by offering a highly efficient and personal service.

For the last ten weeks the Investec High Interest Business Cheque Account (HIBCA) has provided business clients with the opportunity to operate a business bank account that offers free banking and pays a competetive rate of interest.

Investec Bank (UK) Limited is a wholly owned subsidiary of Investec Bank Limited (Investec), a leading independent international investment and private banking group. Investec Bank (UK) is an established private bank, based in the city of London, which offers its private and corporate a range of core banking services.

On the HIBCA account, no charge is levied on the first 80 transactions conducted each calender month (a transaction is defined as a debit or credit entry over the account, and a credit slip may include up to 15 cheques per deposit slip). With a minimum balance of £2001 business clents receive free banking and earn a competitive rate of interest, currently 2.8% gross per annum. To qualify for the HIBCA the minimum balance must be maintained on the account at all times.

HIBCA clients may acquire immediate access to funds via their account cheque books. Should a client make regular withdrawals - to pay bills, for example - standing orders or direct debits may be set up. The HIBCA also provides a regular salary payments system for the convenience of your employees.

Existing Investec Bank (UK) business client - JK Everitt of Flowerkey Systems Limited, Middx says:

"I was struck by how many computer contractors regard paying their bank a fairly hefty fee for the privilege of running their business account as just another unavoidable business expense like tax or accountancy fees.

I opened my business account five years ago with Investec Bank (UK) which not only allows me up to 80 free transactions a month, but also pays me currently a gross interest rate of 2.8% on any credit balance so long as the balance exceeds £2001. For me this amounts to something like £25-£30 per month that the bank pays me instead of me paying them a similar amount each month."

FREE BANKING FOR SUCCESSFUL BUSINESSES

On a minimum operating balance of £2001 you can enjoy the following benefits...

- 60 transactions per month free of charge
- A variable rate of 3.04% AER*
- Standing orders and direct debits may be set up
- No minimum cheque withdrawal or deposit

For more information please call our 24-hour answerphone on 0171 597 4013 or call one of our
Account Managers on 0171 597 4131 between 9am and 5pm Monday to Friday.
Alternatively complete the coupon and FREEPOST it to us.
For your security, telephone calls to Investec Bank (UK) Limited may be recorded.

*The Annual Equivalent Rate (AER) is a notional rate, which illustrates the contractual rate, as if paid and compounded on an annual basis.
Interest is paid on a monthly basis at a reduced rate of 3.00% gross. Interest rates correct as at 30 March 1999. Interest rates may vary.

INVESTEC BANK (UK) LIMITED

To: Investec Bank (UK) Limited, FREEPOST, London EC2B 2AL
Please send me details of the High Interest Business Cheque Account (HIBCA).

Name: _____

Name of Business: _____

Address: _____

_____ Postcode: _____

Investec Bank (UK) Limited, 2 Gresham Street, London EC2V 7QP.
E Mail address: rbd@investec.co.uk

904055

FREE BANKING FOR SMALL BUSINESSES INDEFINITELY

The importance of small business enterprises cannot be underestimated, As the lifeblood of both the UK economy and local communities, small businesses should be given as much encouragement and support as possible.

Recognising this, Abbey National, the UK's fifth largest bank, recently announced free banking for small businesses indefinitely, This announcement, the first move of its kind on the market, could enable many small businesses in the UK to save hundreds of pounds every year.

One small business in two runs their account in credit, and for many their banking needs are usually straightforward. Yet many are forced to pay high charges, demanded by banks who tend to tailor their services towards bigger businesses.

"This is a bold move on the part of Abbey National, it is our way to show our appreciation and support for the small business community," comments Andrew Pople, Managing Director, Retail, Abbey National. "We have found that all too often small businesses are being treated as second-class customers despite the fact they play such a valuable role within local com-

Mr. Andrew Pople, Managing Director, Retail

munities and indeed within the economy as a whole.

"For too long now, small businesses seem to have been at the mercy of the larger commercial banks, often paying significant amounts in transaction charges alone. This latest move is an extension of our policy to offer small businesses a fair and uncomplicated banking relationship."

Abbey National's business and professional banking service, launched last year, initially offered free business banking until the Millennium. The response to the service was so favourable that Abbey National has decided to extend free business banking to 31 December 2000, In addition, for businesses that operate within clearly defined transaction limits, which includes the vast majority of Abbey National's business customers, free business banking will be extended indefinitely,

Abbey National's business and professional banking service is designed to meet the needs of business people who run their accounts in credit and prefer the convenience of doing their banking by telephone and post. Products available include a current account for sole proprietors and two partner businesses and an easy access postal deposit account which is available both to unincorporated and incorporated businesses and institutions in the community. Customers can seek advice by telephone from a team of experienced business bankers with customer administration being provided from the dedicated Business and Professional Banking Centre.

For further information about Abbey National's business and professional banking service, please call free on

0800 056 5151

between 8am - 6pm Monday to Friday.

going to get there. If you have the right controls then the organisation will follow naturally, and in turn you will be able to monitor your plans and see if they are on course and if not, why not. The following financial checklist will set you in the right direction.

FINANCIAL CHECKLIST

Cash control

Day-to-day financial management needs to be applied continuously, and in detail, to the ever changing cycle of expenditure and revenue. In the course of this cycle, cash is converted into trading assets such as stock and work-in-progress, then into debtors and finally back into cash. The cash generated by this process should exceed that which is invested in it, and control is needed to maximise the cycle, to prevent leakage and to ensure that it moves as fast as possible. There follows a series of questions to which you should already know the answers – if you don't, you should find them out.

Cash

- ☐ Have you reviewed security arrangements and insurance?
- ☐ How long is each element of the trading cycle?
- ☐ What changes can be made to improve the cycle?
- ☐ Are budgets expressed both as cash-flow and profit forecasts?
- ☐ Can performance in cash flow be compared with expectations?
- ☐ What is the regular difference between bank statement and cash book?
- ☐ Are bankings sufficiently frequent?
- ☐ Are bank accounts grouped for interest and bank charges purposes?
- ☐ What is the ratio of cash and liquid assets to current liabilities?

Stock and work-in-progress

- ☐ Is stock kept securely and is it adequately insured?
- ☐ Have you taken your accountant's advice on recording and valuation?
- ☐ How much stock is surplus to expected requirements?
- ☐ How many stockouts occur?
- ☐ What is the cost of stockholding?
- ☐ Are reorder quantities established and safety stocks reviewed?
- ☐ How often can you determine stock levels?
- ☐ How much production is for stock or for specific orders?
- ☐ Can stock lines be rationalised?
- ☐ Are bulk orders cost-effective?
- ☐ Do checking procedures prevent under-deliveries or damaged goods being accepted?
- ☐ Can you identify and reduce slow-moving stock?
- ☐ What is the ratio of: stock to purchases?
  - stock to sales?
  - work-in-progress to production?
- ☐ What is the importance/proportion of seasonality and sales trends?

Accounts receivable – debtors

- ☐ What time lag occurs between sales and invoices?
- ☐ Can payment on account or in advance be obtained?
- ☐ Are invoices clear and correct?
- ☐ Can direct debiting or banker's orders be introduced?
- ☐ What is the effect of discounts for prompt payments?
- ☐ Is special clearing of large cheques worthwhile?
- ☐ What about credit insurance?
- ☐ What about debt factoring or invoice discounting?
- ☐ Are customers' credit ratings checked before accepting orders?
- ☐ Is the use of a credit agency justified?
- ☐ Have you considered a debt collection agency?
- ☐ Do you ensure prompt and regular chasing of overdue accounts?
- ☐ What is the ratio of debtors to sales (expressed in days)?

Accounts payable – creditors

- [ ] How many suppliers do you deal with?
- [ ] Are there single source suppliers of key materials?
- [ ] Can payments be delayed?
- [ ] Are buying costs known?
- [ ] Are payment discounts worth taking?
- [ ] Are all purchases properly authorised?
- [ ] Could you pay twice for the same goods?
- [ ] What are the price indices for main supplies?
- [ ] What are the lead times for main suppliers?
- [ ] What is the ratio of: orders overdue to orders placed?
                              creditors to purchases (days)?
                              goods returns to purchases?

Assets employed

- [ ] Can you measure the use of assets in output, value, units?
- [ ] Can you measure contribution from the output?
- [ ] What is maximum capacity?
- [ ] Are there any bottlenecks?
- [ ] What are the fixed costs of the capacity?
- [ ] What is the realisable value of assets employed?
- [ ] Are assets properly insured?
- [ ] Can you time investment or defer taxes?
- [ ] Should you use discounted cash-flow techniques?
- [ ] What are the advantages of buying, hiring or leasing?
- [ ] What is the ratio of: operating profit to operating assets?
                              operating profit to sales?
                              sales to operating assets?
                              actual output to maximum output?
                              unproductive time to total time?

Capital structure

- [ ] What proportion of funds are borrowed and on what terms?
- [ ] Are loans due for early repayment?
- [ ] Are corporate plans prepared?

_____

☐ Are cash-flow forecasts and plans available?
☐ Is liquidity adequate?
☐ Are there special tax considerations?
☐ Have capital markets been explored?
☐ What about the Alternative Investment Market?
☐ What about industrial co-operatives and management buy-
outs?
☐ What is the ratio of: profit before interest to total assets
employed?
borrowed money to equity?
interest payable to borrowed money?

7 Bookkeeping and Administrative Systems

This chapter explains an essential aspect of your business: bookkeeping and administration. It describes a simple and easily kept system of administration and accounts that can be tailored to the needs of most small businesses.

A word of warning – do not try to run before you can walk. Start with simple systems and let them grow with you – your time is extremely valuable and you do not want to find yourself working at an over-complicated system far into the night. You may ask: Why have a system at all? Why keep the books? At the end of the day, the success or failure of your business is not measured primarily in the quality of your product, but in financial terms – in other words, profit. If, for instance, you forget a delivery date or miss invoicing, you will not get cash coming in. A permanent record of your business affairs is therefore required. The Inland Revenue will require its share of your profits, and they will demand – whether or not you have made a profit – financial statements at the end of each year which can be supported by documentary evidence. On these the Inspector of Taxes will base his demands. If the turnover of your business exceeds £51,000 per annum (at present rates), you will have to register with HM Customs and Excise and charge the relevant rate of VAT on your sales. You will be able to set off any VAT charged on incoming invoices against VAT on sales. You will be required to keep adequate records and declare all VAT charged on a regular basis. The VAT inspector may come to check your records. To ensure that your business runs smoothly, you will need to set up systems for ordering and its control, a system for keeping your records in easily accessible files, and personnel records when you take on an employee, etc. All these aspects of your business require systems.

BOOKKEEPING

For your own benefit it is necessary to monitor the well-being of your company, and you will wish to keep a close control of your cash flow and results. One of the major factors that contributes to the failure of many small businesses is a simple lack of financial control. Hard evidence of your trading record will always be required should you find it necessary to raise further capital or even to continue your bank overdraft.

So what does bookkeeping entail and how do you go about it? It is a procedure for recording your business transactions, both receipts and payments, in a way which is easy to understand and makes sure that the information is readily available when you need to refer to it.

The method of recording is designed to take up a minimum amount of your time but still provides a level of control to ensure that you have recorded the information correctly.

If you have set up as a limited company you are required by law to prepare annual accounts which must be audited and filed with Companies House. Even if you are not a company, you will have to prepare accounts for the Inland Revenue each year.

At the end of the year you will probably need to employ an accountant to prepare the actual accounts and submit them to the Inland Revenue. The more time he has to spend on your records the more he will charge you. Any work you can do during the year to write up your own books will save him time and you money.

Of course, each business is different and has its own accounting requirements. The most important thing is to set up a bookkeeping system that can develop with your business. To start off you will require books to record:

☐ an analysis of receipts and payments in your bank account;
☐ your daily take, split, if necessary, into categories;
☐ analysis of miscellaneous cash expenditure, e.g. petty cash;
☐ adequate VAT records;
☐ adequate wages records;
☐ a means of filing invoices, receipts, correspondence, etc.

The first essential is to record the receipts and payments of money – in cash or cheques – in a cash book. For this purpose it is best to use an analysis book which can be purchased from most high street stationers. It has several cash columns, making it easy to analyse types of receipts and payments to individual columns. Take care, however, to choose the right one – compare the suggested rulings shown in the subsequent pages with what is available, and remember it is better to get one with too many columns rather than too few. Ensure that you keep an adequate filing system.

Finally, remember that your accountant, like your bank manager, will prove an invaluable friend to your business. Do not hesitate to consult him and act on his advice when you start. He will have a wealth of experience in dealing with new businesses and five minutes spent with you, even on the telephone, may well save him hours at the end of the year as well as giving him, one hopes, a more successful client.

THE CASH BOOK

The cash book is used to record and analyse all receipts and payments in your bank account. If it is written up regularly it will tell you instantly how much, or how little, money you have in the bank. This is something your bank statement will only tell you when you actually receive it, once a month.

The cash book is divided into two sections. Receipts are entered on the left-hand side and payments on the right. A suggested ruling is shown in Figure 7.1. You will note that there are only five columns of analysis for receipts; this is because your major income will usually be from sales, which can be sub-analysed through the sales day book (Figure 7.2). The sales day book is a record of people who owe you money – your debtors. When you receive payment for the invoices which have been entered, the whole amount of the invoices must be analysed to the 'Debtors' column. Do not separate the VAT in the cash book because this has already been done in the sales day book. Think about the type of receipts you will expect to have in your business and if necessary choose an analysis book with more columns.

When you first start in business you may not require a purchases day book (Figure 7.2) for the analysis of your expenditure; it is often easier to do this analysis in your cash book (Figure 7.1). Hopefully, suppliers will soon grant you credit terms. They will then give you an invoice for your purchases and allow you time, perhaps 30 days, before payment has to be made. You will need to record these invoices in a purchases day book because they represent your creditors. Then you will need a column for 'Creditors' on the payments side of the cash book. When you make your payment remember to enter the whole amount in this column. Do not separate VAT because this will already have been done in the purchases day book. Figure 7.2 shows a typical analysis but you must tailor the headings to suit your own business; your accountant will be able to advise you on this. It cannot be over-emphasised that a detailed breakdown of your expenditure is of great importance to you and your business as well as to your accountant in producing your accounts at the end of the year.

You will note from the headings that sales receipts are itemised by individual invoice; this is by far the best method for small businesses. (When you come to file these invoices away number them in sequence, noting the number in your ledger book. This will make for a quick and easy referral.)

Receipts

As you receive money, either by cheque or in cash, you will want to pay it into your bank account. This you will do by entering such item's details into your paying-in book and presenting

RECEIPTS

Date	Detail	Ref	Bank	VAT	Sales	Debtors	Sundry	
1999 Feb 3	brought fwd		110·20					
5		112	53·85			53·85		
8		113	845·47			845·47		
11		114	126·02			126·02		
11			63·45	9·45	54·00			
12			62·00				62·00	Sale of cabinet
26	B. White	126	147·79			147·78		
	T. Green	127	1127·70			1127·70		
			2536·47	9·45	54·00	2300·32	62·00	
Mar 1	Balance b/d		205·82					

PAYMENTS

Date	Detail	Cheq No.	Ref
1999 Feb 5	Spencer Ltd	012	47
	Brit. Telecom	013	48
16	Alf's Garage	014	49
	Bronkharts	015	50
	Browns	016	51
	Printus Ltd	017	52
17	Ins. Brokers Ltd	018	53
26	A. White	037	
	Inland Revenue	038	
28	Balance c/d		

PAYMENTS (continued)
Assuming that a purchases day book is not being used

Bank	VAT	Creditor	Material	Power	Stationery Post	Tele-phone	Travel exps	Repairs	Rent & Ins	Wages PAYE	HM Customs	Sundry
			*	*	*	*	*	*	*			
63.84	9.50											
167.21	17.17											
35.79	12.78		54.34									
176.25	26.25					150.04						150.00 Accountant
1107.53	164.95		942.58				73.01					
55.42	8.33				47.59							
117.15									117.15			
450.82										450.82		
106.14										106.14		
205.82												
2536.47	233.98		996.92		47.59	150.04	73.01		117.15	556.96		150.00

* These columns will not be needed if you are doing this analysis in a purchase day book.

Figure 7.1 *Cash book*

it and the cheque, or cash, at the bank. Enter the details from the paying-in book into the receipts side of the cash book, recording sales in the sales column, sundry receipts in the sundries column, etc., making sure that all items add across to the total amount entered in the bank column. Remember to separate the VAT from all receipts except for entries in the 'Debtors' column. This should be the amount shown subsequently on your bank statement. If items are credited directly to your bank account you will also have to enter these in your cash book.

Payments

You will draw cheques on your bank account and in the same way you will enter these on the payments side, making sure that the total of the individual cheques and the relevant details are clearly entered. The analysis of the expenditure is then entered into the relevant column. When you are using a purchases day book several of the analysis columns will not be needed in the cash book. If you are registered for VAT you will have to enter the VAT amount in the VAT column leaving only the net amount to be entered in the analysis column except for entries in the 'Creditors' column. Similarly, items appearing directly in your bank statements, such as standing order payments, bank charges, etc., will also have to be entered in your cash book.

Keep a running total of the two bank columns; the difference between the two will give you your bank balance. At the end of each month, total up all the columns and enter the totals. All the subsidiary columns should add back to the two bank columns. If they do not, check your additions and the analysis of your items – five minutes spent now will be amply rewarded in the future. When both sides agree enter the balance to equal up the receipts and payments, and carry this balance forward to the next month.

The bank reconciliation

When you receive your bank statement covering your transactions up to the end of the month, tick off the items, both receipts and payments, in your cash book. In so doing you will find the following items, apart from those which appear in both the statement and your cash book:

- ☐ Receipts and payments not entered in your cash book. Enter these (see example on page 108).
- ☐ Items in your cash book but not in the statements. If these are receipts, check to see whether they have been credited by the bank in the first few days of the next month and list these. If they are cheques they are probably 'outstanding', meaning that it may be some time before the payee of the cheque pays it into his bank and it is presented, through the clearing bank, to your bank. Again, list these.

You can then prepare a reconciliation as shown below.

Bank reconciliation as at 28 February 19—

Balance from bank statement		(455.95)
(overdrawn)		
Add receipts credit 2 March 19—		1,157.00
		701.05
Less outstanding cheques	450.82	
	106.14	
	40.45	597.41
Balance as per cash book		£103.64

If it reconciles, pat yourself on the back. You have probably written your cash book up correctly. It it does not then you will have to look for the difference. Again, do not begrudge the time.

The evidence

As you enter up your cash book, make sure you have some evidence for every entry. On the receipts side it will be your daily takings record, your sales day book (see Figure 7.2) or a note about a sundry receipt. On the payment side it will be the electricity bill, the purchase invoice, the garage bill, etc. Cross reference all these to your cash book and file them in date and number order.

SALES DAY BOOK

Date	Detail	Inv No.	Total	VAT	Net Sales		Amount Paid	Discount	Date Paid	Cheq or Cash
1999 Jan 4	F. Ingram	112	55·23	8·23	47·00		53·85	1·38	3·2·93	Ch
	B. Jones	113	867·15	129·15	738·00		845·47	21·68	6·2·93	Ch
	I. Smith	114	129·25	19·25	110·00		126·02	3·23	8·2·93	Ch
	T. Andrews	115	130·13	19·38	110·75					
5	J. Press	116	448·85	66·85	382·00					
26	B. White	126	151·57	22·57	129·00		147·78	3·79	28·2·93	Ch
	T. Green	127	1207·90	179·90	1028·00		1127·70	30·20	28·2·93	Ch
			7261·20	1081·45	6179·75		2300·82	60·28		

PURCHASES DAY BOOK

This is similar to the sales day book but records all invoices from suppliers for goods or services bought on credit terms. Analyse each invoice according to the type of expense and remember that, when payment of the invoice is recorded in the cash book, the total amount must be entered in the 'Creditor's' column.

Date	Detail	Ref	Total	VAT	Material	Power	Stationery & post	Tele-phone	Travel exps	Motor exps	Date paid

Figure 7.2 Sales day book and purchase day book

The result

The monthly totals for each column will show your expenditure for the month in each category. The monthly figures will make up the annual figures that will appear in your accounts.

SALES DAY BOOK

If your business is in retail, or you only take cash, or if you issue your invoices and collect payment at the same time, it would be simple for you to record your sales directly in the cash book. In this case, you will need a book with a few more columns on the receipts side, according to the detail you need, and, of course, a column for VAT analysis if you are registered. You will not need to keep a separate sales book.

If you do issue invoices in advance (see Figure 7.3) of receiving payment, your cash receipts will not reflect your sales on a daily basis; you therefore need to keep a separate record of the sales invoices that you issue. Use a sales day book for this purpose.

You should keep a record of each invoice you issue. It helps to have printed invoices in sets so that, for instance, the top white copy goes to your customer, the second copy (green) is your accounting copy and is filed in numerical order, and the third copy (blue) goes in the individual customer file. The VAT regulation lays down what information should be shown on an invoice and an example is shown in Figure 7.3 (see page 116).

As you issue your invoice, enter it in your sales day book as shown in Figure 7.2. Again, you will note the individual details shown for each invoice. You have the choice with two or more columns to split your sales between types. Note that the VAT is shown separately and that only the *net* amount is analysed. Make sure you file the copy of the invoice in the same order.

All being well, your customers will pay your invoices, and when they do, enter the amount and date in the columns provided. If you allow them a discount for prompt payment, enter the discount given in the appropriate column so that the amount received plus the discount clears the invoice amount. If your customer settles more than one invoice at a time, cross-reference the receipt to the respective invoices. If you issue credit notes make sure these are entered, placing the details in brackets to show that they should be deducted, in the sales day book.

The receipts entered will form the amounts that are paid into your bank and will be shown in the cash book.

At any time the invoices with no 'paid' entry against them will be those that are unpaid. You will then be in a position to remind the client via a letter, phone call or statement. Similarly after the end of the year, your accountant will be able to pick out those unpaid by the year end by checking the dates of subsequent payment.

Each month, total up the columns and enter the totals, checking that subsidiary columns including VAT balance by adding across to the total. This total will be your monthly sales, including VAT, while your cash book figure will be the cash received from your customers. Any difference will be cash received during the month from invoices issued in the previous month or, conversely, invoices issued but still unpaid.

PETTY CASH BOOK

The petty cash book is used to record small items of expenditure which you pay for in cash. Figure 7.4 (see page 95) illustrates a typical layout for a petty cash book although, again, you must tailor the headings of analysis to suit your business.

Receipts of cash from the bank are shown on the left-hand side and payments on the right-hand side. The easiest method of dealing with petty cash is to draw an initial 'float' of cash for you to hold, preferably in the petty cash box. When any expenditure is made, a petty cash numbered voucher is marked and usually at the end of every week the vouchers are entered in numerical order in the petty cash book. The book is totalled regularly and you then draw a cheque for the total spent in order to 'top up' your float to the original level. Vouchers should always be kept for your accountant at the end of the year and are probably easiest kept in marked envelopes.

The petty cash book should be reconciled monthly so that the balance in the book – the difference between the two sides –

SUPPLIERS

SALES INVOICE NO

54 High Street
Newtown NA2 3QZ
Telephone: 0803 96481

INVOICE ADDRESS		DELIVERY ADDRESS (if different)		

Your Order No	Contract No		Date and Tax Point

Description	Quantity	Price	Tax Exclusive Value	VAT Rate	VAT Payable
			£	%	£

	Tax Exclusive Value	£	%	£
	Plus VAT	£		
	Invoice Value	£		

TERMS OF PAYMENT: 30 days net

VAT No 300 3000 03

Figure 7.3 *Sales invoice*

should equal the money in the box. If it does not you have probably forgotten to enter some item of expenditure. Note that there is a VAT column and that the analysis is net of VAT.

At the end of each month the subsidiary columns are totalled and agreed by adding across to the total column. As with the cash book, the balance is carried forward to the next month.

WAGES BOOK

You will have to keep a wages book and employee records as soon as you start employing others to help you run your business. It is necessary to follow the rules of the Inspector of Taxes and your accountant will assist you in this. It is advisable to arrange all this before you take on any employees so that you will be able to start paying them correctly as soon as they start work.

A new Small Business Service (SBS) to coordinate advice and support for SMEs was announced in the 1999 Budget. The SBS will have a new role helping businesses to comply with regulation and will offer an automated payroll service to new small employers.

The Inspector of Taxes will send you the relevant booklets explaining how income tax and National Insurance contributions are deducted from the wages you pay to your staff and remitted to the Collector of Taxes. The Inspector will also send you stationery on which to record the individual employees' deductions.

In addition to this, you will need a wages book to summarise weekly or monthly payments made. There are several available on the market and Figure 7.5 illustrates a typical layout. It is also necessary to keep personal records of each of your employees, giving:

Full name
Address
Date of birth
National Insurance number
Date of starting work with you
Salary
Position held
Date of leaving if relevant.

Receipts   Payments

Date	Detail	Cash	Date	Detail	Voucher No.	TOTAL	VAT	Post & Stat.	Travel	Motor expense	Clean	Sundries
1999 Feb 1	Balance B/f	270.00	1999 Feb 1	Postage	41	18.00		18.00				
			2	Cleaner	42	8.40					8.40	
				Mr White	43	116.71	8.58	16.03	90.30			1.00 Telephone
			3	Petrol/van	44	11.50	1.50			10.00		
17	Cash book	107.14	4	Greers Ltd	45	.63						63 Coffee
			10	Mr Smith	46	171.86	22.43	149.43				
			Feb 28	Total		326.10	32.31	18.00/165.46	90.30	10.00	8.40	1.63
				Balance		165.12						
26	Cash book	114.08				491.22						
		491.22										
March 1	Balance	165.12										

Figure 7.4 Petty cash book

You will need to give your employees payslips which detail how their wages are made up. You will also need to keep records of your employees' absences due to illness and you are required to compute and pay to them sickness pay, which may then be reclaimed from your payment to the Collector of Taxes. This is called Statutory Sick Pay and the Inspector of Taxes will furnish you with all relevant forms and documents regarding this; since April 1994 the refund is only available for employers whose National Insurance bill for the year is less than £20,000. (Chapter 10 discusses the details of recruitment and employment law.)

Irrespective of whether you pay your staff weekly or monthly, you will need to draw a cheque or cash to pay them. This will be entered in the cash book or petty cash book as will the cheque drawn to remit to the Inland Revenue for the PAYE and National Insurance deductions. Note that the employer also contributes to National Insurance.

Summarise your wages book and check that the figures agree with the wages column of your cash book. The figure that will appear in your accounts will be the gross cost of the wages, that is, the net amount paid to employees plus the PAYE and National Insurance deducted, plus the employer's contribution. The wages book should give you the breakdown of this figure.

Individual entries should agree with the tax deduction cards supplied by the Inland Revenue. Wages envelopes with a printed summary on the outside are readily available. If you have more than a few employees it is probably a good idea to look at one of the proprietary systems which allow you to deal with the payslips, wages book and deduction card all at the same time.

Remember that if your business is a limited company and you are a director, even if you are the sole director or jointly with your wife, any money taken from the firm will be your wages and should be taxed through the PAYE (Pay As You Earn) system. The Inland Revenue is now quite strict about this and will penalise directors for drawing untaxed lump sum amounts.

If you are a sole trader or partnership, your tax is assessed on your real results and the amounts you take are your drawings. These do not have to be taxed at the time, but remember that you are still liable to pay National Insurance and will have to pay, depending on your results, tax on your profits in the future.

Month Ending _FEB 99_ Week No. _____

| NAME | National Insurance No | Contribution Table Letter | Gross Amount Due | EMPLOYER'S DEDUCTIONS | | | Net Amount Due | EMPLOYER'S CONTRIBUTIONS |
				Tax	Class 1			Class 1
A. White (Code 220L)	YK021219B	A	636.07	135.82	57.42		443.05	66.67

Figure 7.5 *Wages book*

VALUE ADDED TAX (VAT)

For most small businesses, the VAT return is relatively easy to complete, always given that your books are kept up to date and totalled on a regular basis. If you have followed the advice of the earlier parts of this chapter then you will have already recorded all the details necessary for completing the VAT return.

It is advisable to keep a separate book for your VAT workings. Figure 7.6 gives an example of this. The information in the official VAT return is in the VAT column of the book and in the 'totals excluding VAT' columns. Do be especially careful not to claim in the input column any VAT paid over to HM Customs and Excise. This is a very common mistake; unfortunately they do not take kindly to you boosting your income by claiming back the VAT already paid over. VAT is discussed in detail in the following chapter.

CREDIT CONTROL

This area is very important to the continued success of your business. It relies on information found in the sales book and cash book previously covered.

What are your terms of credit? And how long do your clients take to pay? Are you currently overdrawn at the bank and still owed outstanding monies?

It is a fallacy to believe that applied credit control will upset your customers. What is the point of selling your product if you are not going to get paid? If done in a proper and efficient way, credit control is not only effective but will not offend your clients. They will respect you for it as they in turn have to do the very same thing.

Do not be heavy handed. Your first action should be a statement of account sent out between 14 days and 21 days after the invoice (or with an existing credit chasing system) or at the end of every month. After a reasonable period of time, a pleasant telephone call to your customer's 'bought ledger' department should gain some response. Again allow a few weeks to elapse and then if nothing happens send a polite letter as a reminder that the account is now overdue by 'XX' days and that you would appreciate prompt settlement of the outstanding amount. A rapport often builds up between yourself and the 'bought ledger' and if this is kept on a pleasant business footing then you can succeed in calling in outstanding money where a hard-handed approach will often fail to win prompt action. You should not, unless it is absolutely necessary, resort to solicitors' letters. Should recovery, after completing the credit-chasing procedure, become difficult you can try to reclaim the debt by issuing a summons in the small claims section of the County Court. However, the recent introduction of legislation does now allow for interest to be added to unpaid invoices of over 30 days.

After some time a pattern will emerge showing you the clients who pay promptly and those who take longer to settle their account. Large firms will often take 60 to 90 days to settle, sometimes longer than that, so do ensure that this is taken into account or, if not acceptable, that the matter is discussed in advance with your client and credit terms agreed.

If a client is consistently overdue in paying your invoices, to the extent of using between 60 and 90 days over and above the credit term agreed, then you should consider whether or not to withdraw credit terms or to cease trading with them. This decision, of course, rests entirely with you and should not be taken lightly. If either eventuality occurs, make clear to your client the reason why the step has had to be taken.

If you allow a discount for prompt payment ensure that, should the client not pay within the time, the discount is not deducted from the paid invoiced amount.

ADMINISTRATIVE SYSTEMS

This section is based on administrative principles vital to the success of an existing or proposed small business. It also assumes that you know in detail the product or service of your business.

Paperwork and legislative controls hold little attraction for many people – indeed, most would tell you that they hate paperwork –

but they are essential to the success of a business. These controls do not have to be either time-consuming or sophisticated.

Earlier in the book you will have read about how to obtain additional finance, whether or not it is best to operate in a partnership or as a sole trader, and rules on sales and marketing. Basically, in operating your business you will have three main factors to consider:

☐ the knowledge of your product/service;
☐ money;
☐ people.

Each of these areas requires records and administrative procedures of one sort or another to comply with statutory or just sound business requirements.

Simple systems

Financial

The first area to examine when implementing systems is the financial one. If you go to a bank for additional funds the first thing you will be asked is, 'How soon can you pay it back?' and/or 'Can you let me have a cash-flow statement?' This cash-flow statement is a vital part of your administrative records. It must project for at least a year ahead, preferably three years, and it must show what bills you expect to receive month by month for rent, rates, light and heating purchases, wages, even VAT. You must then estimate the volume of your sales receipts over the same period – remember to be realistic when working on future projections. Then and only then can you estimate what your cash balance or overdraft figure is likely to be at the end of each month. Naturally, any hire purchase, leasing or loan repayments must be similarly noted.

Accounts records should be kept and an explanation of what books to keep and how to keep them has already been given. You must remember to set aside time to keep these accounts up to date and accurate, otherwise the entire accounts system will grind to a halt.

For VAT RETURN – quarter ended ....   For quarter ended ....

	Month Feb 99 £	Month £	Month £	TOTAL £	Month £	Month £	Month £	TOTAL £

OUTPUT TAX

	Month Feb 99 £	Month £	Month £	TOTAL £	Month £	Month £	Month £	TOTAL £
Sales	1081·45							
Cash	·							
Bank	9·45							
	1090·90							

INPUT TAX

	Month Feb 99 £	Month £	Month £	TOTAL £	Month £	Month £	Month £	TOTAL £
Purchases	-							
Cash	32·31							
Bank	238·98							
	271·29							

NET Payable
TAX Receivable

NET Payable
TAX Receivable

OUTPUT (excluding VAT)

Sales	6179·75							
Cash	–							
Bank	2527·02							
	8706·77							

INPUT (excluding VAT)

Purchases	–							
Cash	293·79							
Bank	2297·49							
	2591·28							

Figure 7.6 *VAT summary*

Stock levels

An area often forgotten is your existing stock level. This stock represents money tied up and not available for use. Whether it is for your own use or for resale, what is the level of your stock? Stock records, kept up to date, can tell you what the present level of stock is, with the added bonus that they can also tell you the length of time the stock has been held and the quantities, and you can then do something about it where necessary. If you review stock records regularly, you can see a glance what is moving and what is not, and this can be a great help in controlling the capital outlay necessary when keeping stock up to the right level. Again you need a simple card index showing commodity, pack, supplier, minimum and maximum stock, incomings and outgoings, and balance with a value column.

Personnel

Another area of administration to look at is personnel. All details relating to your employees must be assigned a file – one file for each individual. All appropriate records must be kept in this file, such as job application forms, references, your copy of the contract of employment, letter of appointment, etc. These files must be kept private and confidential and noted as such. Notes from discussions should also be filed away and any letters of complaint too. Wages cards (and your account files and books) can also be kept in the private and confidential filing drawer as this will save on space initially.

Keep copies to hand of the different leaflets given out by the Department for Education and Employment and the Department of Social Security.

The key to good administration is to keep it simple, creating a file only if you really need it. A correspondence filing system is the most basic and the easiest to start; all you need to do is put one client's correspondence in one file, that of another client in the next file, and so on. You then build up these files and put them away alphabetically. Your business administration files should be divided into six parts – office, personnel, legal, accounting, equipment (purchases) and sales (customers). Keep the files separate at all times, preferably in a safe, fireproof location. Do consider keeping duplicate records. Should any unforeseen accident occur, such as a fire, it would take some time to compile replacement documentation. Consider purchasing a safe in which to place your valuables. Your office insurance payments could be reduced should you acquire a safe.

A first-aid kit will have to be purchased and a first-aid system set up. It is extremely important that your office and/or factory complies with the Health and Safety at Work Act. The Department for Education and Employment will send you all the necessary details; you may already have had a visit from your local factory inspector to ensure that you are complying with the Act. A book will need to be kept to record any accidents.

What about office equipment – should you buy or lease it? If you are a new company starting up you could find leasing difficult to obtain. On the other hand, if you purchase, you are allowed to write off part of the value of the machine each year. As there are so many different machines, at varying prices, it is often best to look at the situation carefully in the light of your own requirements and business. If you are thinking about buying a computer, shop around and decide what sort of work you want the machine to do. However, unless you have a manual system up and working it is pointless trying to match an existing computer program to take over the existing workload. You must know what you need and want from a system before you buy it. Many companies have run into serious administrative difficulties (and financial ones too) over the purchase of a computer. Telegraph Publications have produced a comprehensive book on the subject entitled *How to Choose and Use Business Microcomputers and Software* which will be most helpful.

Part of successful administration is making sure that your business is covered by insurance. Obtain quotations and compare the price and content of different policies as they vary, and do read the small print. You are required by law to have a policy called 'Employer's Liability' and the policy must be displayed in a prominent position. Your machinery, premises, vehicles, etc., will all need to be covered by insurance.

Administration is just as important an ingredient in the success of a business as the rest of the business disciplines. To run a business you have to amalgamate the various skills involved, and you will find that at any one time one particular skill will be needed more than the others. But remember that clear and simple administrative systems will ensure that you will not run foul either of the law, the various government departments or your customers.

The list of further reading in Appendix II is a useful reference should you wish to locate a book that goes into more detail on a specific business or financial topic.

Checklist: Preparing finance and administration

☐ Have you set up your bookkeeping system?
☐ Have you considered and set up a credit control system?
☐ What other business controls have you set up?
☐ Are you aware of tax, including VAT, and National Insurance requirements?
☐ Are you aware of welfare and health & safety regulations?
☐ What special paperwork is necessary?
☐ What records and filing must be arranged?
☐ Will you require telephone, telex or fax services?
☐ What else should be considered in your case?

Checklist: Purchasing

☐ Do you know how much stock to buy, when to buy it and at what cost?
☐ What will unsold stock cost you?
☐ Can you store your purchases securely?
☐ Have you prepared a stock control system?
☐ Have you sought several quotations for supply (in writing)?
☐ Have you planned to keep all expenditure to a sensible minimum?

Source: *DfEE, Running your own Business*

---

8 National Insurance, Income Tax, Corporation Tax and VAT

'No man in this country is under the smallest obligation, moral or otherwise, so to arrange his legal relations to his business or to his property as to enable the Inland Revenue to put the largest possible shovel into his stores.'

This was Lord President Clyde's view, adding that the taxpayer is 'entitled to be astute to prevent, so far as he honestly can, the depletion of his means by the Revenue'.

When you start your business, you have to decide the form it is going to take: sole trader, partnership, unlimited liability or limited liability company. The tax position can decide which form you start off with, although no good tax adviser will ignore the commercial requirements. But just a slight adjustment here and there can make a material difference to the amount of tax that you pay – and not only to the amount but also to when it is paid. At the end of this chapter you will find an invaluable checklist of the key points which you need to know about tax and your business. (While every effort has been made to ensure that the figures given in this chapter are correct, please refer to the latest DSS and Inland Revenue leaflets for the most up-to-date figures.)

NATIONAL INSURANCE

Although we talk of National Insurance (NI) as 'contributions', it is, of course, just another form of taxation. NI is easy for the government to levy as it is an efficient system of collecting tax; it does not cause too much aggravation or need many staff to administer it.

National Insurance is often the forgotten element in tax planning. The amount involved these days can be quite considerable and it can tip the balance when you are trying to decide whether or not to set up as a sole trader, partnership, or whether to start off straight away as a limited liability company. One practical point to remember when employing additional staff is that the employer, in addition to deducting NI from that person, also has to pay to the government its own NI contribution for that employee.

NI: AN OUTLINE

The employed

Class 1 contributions are in general payable by employees over the age of 16. Contributions are normally paid by the employee and the employer. However, if the employee has reached pensionable age (65 for men, and 60 for women) only the employer has to pay the contributions. Employers are required to deduct contributions from the employee's pay and to pay over the total to the Inland Revenue along with income tax deducted under the PAYE scheme.

☐ Rates of contribution are expressed as a percentage of earnings where these are at present between the 'earnings limits', which are in turn expressed in weekly, monthly or yearly terms to be used according to the normal pay intervals of the employee. Earnings limits and the new NI Class 1 rates are as shown in Tables 8.1 and 8.2.

☐ No contributions are payable if earnings are below the lower earnings limit subject to rules for persons with more than one employment.

- ☐ Where earnings fall in a particular bracket, contributions are payable at the rates indicated for that bracket on the full amount of the employee's earnings.
- ☐ Where the employer has an occupational pension scheme which satisfies certain requirements, he can 'contract out' of the state scheme. The full rates apply to the part of the earnings up to the lower earnings limit but there is a reduced rate for the part of the earnings in excess of that figure.
- ☐ Earnings for contribution purposes are gross earnings before PAYE or pension fund deductions, but do not include redundancy payments, payments in lieu of notice, termination payments, pensions, benefits in kind, meal vouchers, expenses or tips not paid by the employer.
- ☐ Primary contributions due from an employee with more than one employment in one year are limited to a maximum of the full rate applied to 53 weeks times the weekly upper earnings limit. There is normally no limit on the employer's contributions.
- ☐ There are special rules for persons entering or leaving the country. These may be modified if the movement is between EU countries or between Great Britain and a country with whom it has a reciprocal agreement.

The self-employed

- ☐ Self-employed persons over 16 and under 65 (men) or 60 (women) can be liable to pay flat-rate Class 2 contributions and earnings-related Class 4 contributions. There are exemptions from Class 2 contributions, the most important being if profits (as shown by the accounts) are expected to be below £3,770 (for 1999/2000).
- ☐ The rate of the Class 2 contribution is £6.55 per week. Contributions may be paid by direct debit through a bank account or Giro. The option of payment by purchasing stamps is no longer available.
- ☐ Earnings-related Class 4 contributions for any year are based on the profit assessable under Schedule D Class I or II for that year, after taking account of capital allowances, balancing

Table 8.1 *Contracted in on all earnings. NI Class 1 contributions from 6 April 1999*

Earnings per week	Employees (Rate applying to all earnings)		Employers (Rate applying to all earnings)
	On first £66	*Remainder*	
up to £66.00	0	0	0
£66.00 to £83.00	0%	10%	0%
£83.00 to	0%	10%	12.2%
£500.00	no additional liability		12.2%

Table 8.2 *Contracted out on all earnings. NI Class 1 contributions from 6 April 1999*

Earnings per week	Employees (Rate applying to all earnings)		Employers (Rate applying to all earnings)	
			Remainder	
	On first £66	*Remainder*	*Salary-related*	*Money-purchased*
up to £66.00	0	0	0	0
£66.00 to £83.00	0%	8.4%	0	0%
£83.00 to £500.00	0%	8.4%	2.0%	11.6%
over £500.00	no additional liability		4.0%	12.2%

charges, loss relief, and annual payments incurred for trading purposes. For 1999/2000 the rate of contribution is 6 per cent on assessable profits between £7,530 and £26,000 per annum. The businessman can no longer obtain 50 per cent relief for income tax purposes on his graduated Class 4 contributions.

☐ Class 4 contributions are collected along with income tax on the Schedule D Class I or II assessment.

_____

☐ Where a person is both employed and self-employed, his total maximum contribution under NI Classes 1, 2 and 4 is equal to 53 weekly Class 1 contributions on the upper earnings limit at the standard rate.

The unemployed

☐ Class 3 contributions are entirely voluntary and are payable by those who wish to secure a measure of entitlement to benefits and whose contribution record is not otherwise good enough. Class 3 contributions can only be paid by a person who has not paid, in Class 1 or 2, contributions equal to 52 Class 1 contributions at the standard rate on the lower weekly earnings limit.

☐ The rate is £6.45 per week. Contributions are paid by direct debit through a bank Giro or account.

CONTRIBUTIONS

The rates of Class 1 NI contributions effective from 6 April 1999 are as shown in Table 8.1.

You will see that, up to £500 per week, these rates apply to all earnings, and this can have an adverse effect where an employee is paid on or just above the level where the rates change. If you were to pay someone £68 per week both you and that person would be liable to Class 1 on the whole of that person's earnings, so an extra £2 per week can lead to a reduction in take-home pay for your employee and an increase in overheads for you. At the other end of the scale, although an employee does not have to pay contributions on any earnings above £500 per week (£26,000 a year), his employer is liable for NI at 10 per cent on all the employee's earnings without limit.

If you or your employees are contracted out of the state pension scheme, you pay at reduced rates on the amount of salary over the lower earnings limit. The applicable rates effective since 6 April 1999 are shown in Table 8.2.

The benefits available to the self-employed through their Class 2 and 4 contributions are a great deal less than those to which employees and directors are entitled through their Class 1 contributions.

BUSINESS TAX

For the individual

If you go into business as an individual or in partnership, your profits will be assessed for income tax. If you choose to operate through a UK limited liability company you will be liable to pay corporation tax (CT) on the chargeable profits of that company.

If you are a sole trader or partnership setting up business, you are entitled to count as part of your trading expenses any revenue expenditure incurred by you in connection with the business for up to seven years before you actually started trading (or five years if you started trading before 5 April 1995). For example, you may own a workshop for some three to six months before starting any work in it. But you are going to be paying rent, and you may have other outgoings such as gas and electricity. You can offset those against the income that you eventually generate when you do start trading. Those expenses, plus, for example, capital allowances, can normally be used to reduce your profit or generate an income tax loss if you are setting up on your own. If you make an income tax loss then there are all sorts of things that you can do with the loss: you can carry it forward against the future income from your trade; if you have other income in the same year in which you

Table 8.3 *NI contributions Classes 2 and 4 self-employed 1999/2000*

Class 2 fixed per week	
no liability if earning below £3,770	£6.55
Class 4 earnings related	
on profits between £7,530 and £26,000 a year	6.0%

make the loss, then you can set that loss off immediately against the other income.

Furthermore, if you make an income tax loss in the first four years of trading, it can be carried back and set off against your other income in the three years prior to the loss. However, if you have a capital loss on a chargeable asset, you can set that off against capital gains in the same period or you can carry that capital loss forward. But you *cannot* set a capital loss against income – that is a basic rule of revenue law.

If you are an established self-employed person, whether working as a sole trader or as a partner, the system running until 1995/96 was that you paid tax on what was known as the preceding year basis. However, new income tax rules came into play in the tax year 1997/98. From 9 April 1997, the existing 'preceding year' basis was replaced by the 'current year' basis. This means that tax is assessed on the profit of the accounting year that ends in the tax year itself (current year), rather than the profit of the accounting year that ends in the previous tax year. Tax is paid on 31 January in the tax year and 31 July of the next tax year.

For your company

For companies it is a lot simpler. They just pay tax on a current year basis, on whatever they earn in the particular accounting period. Companies pay corporation tax (CT) on both income and capital gains (Table 8.4).

You calculate your trading income on normal accounting principles. In other words, not on a cash basis but on an invoicing basis, so you count the income when you become entitled to it rather than when you actually receive the cash. Similarly with expenditure, you bring in the liability when it arises, not when you pay out the money. Trading income is the only type of income dealt with on that basis; most other income is dealt with on a receipts basis.

For most companies the date of payment for corporation tax will generally be nine months after the end of the accounting period. If the companies receive income from which income tax has been deducted they are given credit for that, and it is set off

Table 8.4 *Corporation tax*

	Accounting period commencing 1 April			
	1999	1998	1997	1996
Full rate	30%	31%	31%	33%
Small companies rate	20%	21%	21%	24%
Charged up to	£300,000	£300,000	£300,000	£300,000
Marginal relief up to	£1,500,000	£1,500,000	£1,500,000	£1,500,000
Marginal rate	32.5%	33.5%	33.5%	35.25%
Small companies' fraction	Abolished	1/40	1/40	9/400
Advance CT	Abolished	1/4	1/4	1/4

against the corporation tax due. If they have no profits liable for CT, they get the income tax back.

What are your allowances?

Once you have calculated your total profits, there are certain things you can deduct. The main element is non-bank interest paid for business purposes. If you pay interest to someone other than a bank, it is allowed not against your trading income but against your total profits. So, if you knock off the non-banking interest, you arrive at the profit chargeable for CT.

Marginal small companies' relief

Below £300,000 profits you pay 20 per cent and over £1,500,000 you pay 30 per cent in 1999/2000. In between these two amounts is the 'marginal small companies' relief'. This is an effective tax rate of 32.5 per cent for year ending 31 March 1999. For a family company, making profits slightly over £300,000, it may be worth paying out extra cash to, say, directors' bonuses. In addition, it is worth taking on a little more plant and equipment and paying in a little more to the company's pension scheme in order to stay out of this £300,000 plus band, which results in you paying CT at 32.5 per cent on the difference between £300,000 and £1,500,000.

The limits of £1,500,000 and £300,000 are reduced if you have more than one company under your control, or more than one company in a group of companies. It would be very nice, of course, if you were making £500,000, just to set up four companies, with £125,000 profits at 20 per cent tax on each. However, it does not work that way.

What are dividends?

In small companies the shareholders and directors are usually the same. If you have any surplus profits they can be allocated as directors' bonuses, in which case they will count as earned income. If, however, you take out the cash as a dividend, you will not get a deduction from the profits in respect of the amounts that you pay out, which you do with the director's bonus.

What about salaries?

In a company, when you pay yourself a salary, which is taxable in your hands, it is a deduction as far as the company is concerned. From the point of view of the company, directors' salaries and bonuses are an allowable deduction because they are going to be taxed in the hands of the recipient.

One important aspect now is that dividend payments do *not* attract NI contributions whereas salary and bonuses do and these can be quite costly. Where the shareholders and directors of a company are one and the same, it may be worth paying out a part of their 'reward' by way of dividend instead of remuneration. Where the company is paying corporation tax at the 20 per cent rate, this change makes no effective difference to its tax position, but could lead to a useful saving of NI contributions.

There are a number of other factors, however; the timing of tax payments, effect on pension scheme contributions and social security benefits, valuation of the company's shares – all these factors need to be taken into consideration. Each situation needs to be looked at on its own merits and professional advice is strongly recommended before any decision is taken.

WHAT ARE CAPITAL ALLOWANCES?

Capital allowances can also be deducted from trading income provided they have been incurred before the end of the accounting period. While you are not allowed to deduct depreciation in arriving at your taxable income, you are allowed instead to deduct capital allowances. These are given on a wide range of capital expenditure, for example, plant and machinery, industrial and agricultural buildings, with special treatment available for 'short-life' assets. In some cases, it does not matter whether the asset is in use or not; provided that the expenditure has been incurred, the business will qualify for relief.

Allowances on plant and machinery

There has never been a definition of plant and machinery but the term encompasses not only machines, but also many fixtures and fittings, office equipment and motor vehicles.

The allowance generally available is a 25 per cent 'writing down' allowance. This is given on the 'pool' of expenditure calculated on a reducing balance basis. Expenditure on new assets is added to the pool and the proceeds of plant disposed of are deducted from the pool so as to arrive at the amount on which the 25 per cent allowance is given. If the accounting period is less than 12 months, the allowance is reduced accordingly.

For expenditure between 2 July 1999 and 1 July 2000 an initial allowance of 40 per cent of the cost can be claimed on certain expenditure.

Special treatment is given to motor-cars costing more than £12,000: the writing down allowance on each such car is limited to a maximum of £3,000 a year.

Allowances on industrial buildings

If you buy an industrial building or have it built for use in your own trade or to lease to someone else in their trade, you may be entitled to capital allowances on the building. That amount of allowance will depend on whether the building is new or second-hand when you acquired it. If the building is new you may claim an annual 'writing down' allowance of 4 per cent on the cost of the building, but not the land. If you buy a second-hand building, you may be entitled to 'writing down' allowances but the level of these will depend upon the allowances claimed by the vendor of the building. If you buy a new commercial building in an Enterprise Zone, you are entitled to an initial allowance of 100 per cent. You need not claim this allowance in full; instead, should you wish, you can claim a 25 per cent 'straight line' allowance on the balance in subsequent years.

If you sell an industrial building, part or even all of the allowances you have claimed may be clawed back, ie added to your income, depending upon the price you receive for the building and when the expenditure in respect of which the allowances were claimed was originally incurred.

Relief for trading losses

- ☐ These can be set against other income or chargeable gains of the same or the preceding accounting year.
- ☐ Relief can be carried forward against future trading profits on the same trade.
- ☐ On cessation of trade the losses of the last 12 months can be carried back against trading profits of the three previous years.

Capital gains

- ☐ The gains on the disposal of business assets can be deferred if another business asset is acquired with the proceeds, though normally not more than one year earlier or three years later. This is known as 'rollover relief'.
- ☐ Capital losses can be set off against capital gains in the same accounting period, and net losses can be carried forward to future periods.
- ☐ Capital losses cannot be set against income.

What is a close company?

Most small companies will be what are known as 'close companies', defined as being controlled by five or fewer shareholders or by any number of directors who are also shareholders. The vast majority of companies in this country are close companies. Bearing in mind that you can still pay 40 per cent tax on your own income, it would be very handy to put some money into a company and leave it to grow, knowing that the bulk of it will never pay more than 20 per cent tax.

The Inland Revenue was aware of this dodge of using companies as money boxes to hold cash that would have been paying tax at fairly high rates as individuals' income, and there is a 30 per cent CT charge on close investment companies which retain most of their profit.

Furthermore, if your company pays tax at 20 per cent, you do not want to take the money out of the company and pay tax on it. You just borrow it from the company and carry on borrowing larger and larger amounts and never pay back the sums borrowed. But the Revenue have spotted this loophole too. Now, when a shareholder receives such a loan, the company has to put on deposit with the Collector of Taxes the equivalent of the recently abolished Advance Corporation Tax (ACT) so the loan is treated virtually as a dividend. In addition, the recipient could be assessed to income tax on the benefit of the loan. The annual benefit would be equal to the amount of deemed interest on the loan at the 'official rate' (6.75 per cent since 6 November 1996).

There are stringent rules under the Directors and Insolvency Act 1985 which have particular relevance for close companies and their director-shareholders. Under this Act anyone who acts as a director is considered to be a director and is personally liable for any debts arising should the company continue to trade while insolvent. (The definition of director includes shadow directors, non-executive directors, etc.) The Act does not allow for the excuse of incompetence or lack of knowledge, and assumes that directors must be responsible for their actions and those of their companies. In certain circumstances directors can be jointly liable for the actions of fellow directors. Financial implications aside, should a director fail to fulfil the administrative obligations as laid out in the Companies Act and the Insolvency Act 1986, fines as well as imprisonment can be enforced. Directors can also be disqualified from acting as a director for up to 15 years. Careful study of this Act is therefore advised.

Running costs

Now that the corporation tax rate for small companies has been reduced to 20 per cent, tax alone should not be a reason to stop you from incorporating the business. But you have to remember that if you do this you may have to have an annual statutory audit which entails paying an audit fee. Generally speaking, the running costs of a limited liability company are higher than those of a trading business, and this should be borne in mind. And although it is called a limited liability company, you may not get the full benefit of limited liability because nobody will advance a small company money unless the director-shareholders put up personal guarantees.

You should also remember that as the company and its shareholders are separate legal entities, a double charge to capital gains tax can arise if the shareholders wish to realise the assets in the company. First, there may be a charge within the company to corporation tax on the gain arising on the disposal of the assets concerned by the company. Second, there may be a further charge to capital gains tax on the gain arising to the shareholders when they realise their shares, for example, on liquidating the company.

On the other hand, where an individual disposes of his business or sells his shares in his family trading company when he is over 50 or is obliged to retire under that age through ill health, he may be able to claim substantial relief, up to as much as £250,000, against the chargeable gains arising on him in this way.

VALUE ADDED TAX (VAT)

VAT is charged by most businesses on all sales and the tax collected is paid over to HM Customs and Excise quarterly. A business can usually claim a set-off for VAT which it has paid. Small businesses may not be liable to register, but this means that they cannot recover it either.

Where a business is exempt – the major ones are property investment, banking and insurance services – VAT is not charged but the business cannot recover VAT which it pays.

Where the turnover limits are not likely to be exceeded, a business can, in certain circumstances, still register. This may be advantageous, particularly if supplies are being made to other taxable businesses which can recover VAT charged. It is only by registering that the VAT paid can be recovered. Also, where a business intends to make sales subject to VAT at some time in the future, it may be allowed to register as an 'intending trader' (subject to certain conditions imposed by Customs and Excise) so as to be able to recover VAT on its expenses in the meantime. It is also possible for a newly registered business to reclaim VAT on goods bought prior to registration where these are still held at that time and on services supplied to it for up to six months prior to registration.

You should be aware that VAT on certain expenses is not recoverable: the most notable example is entertaining customers or suppliers and the cost of buying (but not running) motor cars.

Registration for VAT requires extra record-keeping, but this should not be significant unless the business is using one of the special schemes for antiques and certain second-hand goods under which VAT is only charged on the margin between cost and selling price, and not on the whole selling price. There is also a variety of schemes for calculating the VAT liability of a retail business.

As the payment of VAT can handicap the entrepreneur starting off in business, when compiling sales forecasts it is advisable, should they show that the VAT limit is going to be exceeded, to allow for the relevant amounts of VAT in the overall forecast. Forewarned is forearmed. Leaflets on VAT can be obtained from your local Customs and Excise office.

Registration

You do not charge VAT unless your annual turnover exceeds £51,000. It is important to register promptly if:

☐ at the end of any month the value of your taxable supplies in the past 12 months has exceeded £51,000; or

☐ at any time there are reasonable grounds for believing that the value of taxable supplies you will make in the next 30 days will exceed £51,000.

The VAT inspector will want tax on your sales from the date of your registration. If you do not register in time, he will still want to collect tax from the date you should have registered, and will not allow you to set off the VAT on expenses incurred during the intervening period.

It is possible to register voluntarily. This is particularly useful if you make mainly zero-rated supplies because it enables you to get back the VAT you have paid out. Most supplies attract VAT at the standard rate of 17.5 per cent but certain categories are zero-rated, i.e. there is no VAT payable, and these include most foods, books and newspapers, transport, and children's clothing. Export of goods and many supplies of services to foreigners are also 'zero-rated' or 'exempt' categories. Domestic fuel attracts VAT at 5 per cent. The only person who suffers VAT, and this is the usual peculiar approach of most tax legislation, is someone who is exempt from it. It might be the ordinary citizen, or someone in the property business, or bankers, but whoever is exempt cannot reclaim VAT despite having paid it out.

Companies register separately, but if they are part of a group or commonly controlled they can register together. For unincorporated businesses it is the proprietor of the business who has to register and all his business activities are looked at together. So if he has a turnover of £20,000 a year on a fruit stall in the local market and another £32,000 as a consultant, he must charge VAT on the lot as it is over the £51,000 limit. This does mean keeping records and in recognition of this there are special schemes available to small traders.

The payment of VAT due on a cash accounting system is widely publicised by HM Customs and Excise. This optional system benefits businesses which have a turnover of up to £350,000 per year. Late payment of invoices in the past has left small businesses with an extremely vulnerable cash-flow situation. Now these businesses do not have to pay VAT until the related invoices have been paid.

In addition, there is also an option of annual accounting for VAT, up to an annual turnover limit of £300,000. Under this scheme, businesses have to complete only one VAT return per year; however, there will be nine *advance* payments on account to be made.

The period regarding registration for VAT purposes is 30 days.

Bad debt relief of VAT can be claimed after six months if the debt has been written off in the business's accounts.

WHAT TAX CHOICES DO YOU HAVE?

For the sole trader

Let us suppose that you are in a fortunate position in that your pretax profits after capital allowances and all the other things (but not remuneration for yourself, as you are not incorporated) are £70,000. Let us take the example of a small businessman who is married. As a sole trader he is entitled to the married couple's allowance. In 1999/2000 he pays income tax of £20,968.60, Class 2 contributions of £340.60 and Class 4 contributions of £1108.20. His total contribution to the Exchequer is £22,417.40.

For the partnership

If he formed or was part of a partnership, our businessman could take his wife into equal partnership and her share of the income would be taxed separately. If this is done each would earn £35,000. He will get the married couple's allowance and each would get the personal allowance. He would pay tax of £6968.60, Class 2 contributions of £340.60 and Class 4 contributions of £1108.20. She would pay tax of £7311.00 and would also pay Class 2 contributions of £340.60 and Class 4 contributions of £1108.20.

The total for both is £17,177.20 which shows a reduction of £5,240.20 when compared with the sole trader example. However, the wife must genuinely work in the business in a capacity likely to earn the sum of money being paid.

If you are starting a business, never set up as a husband and wife; make sure that one or other is an employee for the first year, as your first year's accounts usually form the basis of assessment for the first three tax years. The earnings of an employee are only taxed in one year so if one of you is an employee for that first year you pay tax on those earnings once, but the employer gets the deduction two and a half to three times over. Often it is the husband who sets up on his own and takes the wife as the employee and then the wife is introduced as a partner at the end of the first year.

For the company

Let us suppose our married couple choose to incorporate and form a limited company. The company has £70,000 of taxable profits before they draw anything out of their business to live on. Let us assume they each take a salary of £20,000. Income tax on that for 1999/2000 works out at £3211.07 for the husband and £3407.95 for the wife. Class 1 NI is £1656.80 from each employee plus the company's contribution of £1913.45 per employee. The company is going to pay 20 per cent of what is left, that is £70,000 less £40,000 salaries less £3826.90 employer's NI contribution, which equals £26,173.10. Corporation tax at 20 per cent on this is £5234.62 making a total contribution to the Exchequer of £18,994.14 against a total of £17,177.20 for the partnership.

Benefits in kind ('perks')

One of the advantages of the company structure is that it is possible to provide employees (in particular the directors) with various tax-efficient benefits in kind. These are likely to give rise to some additional tax on the individual, based on the value of the benefit that he receives, but the cost of this is likely to be significantly less to him than if he had to provide this benefit entirely at his own expense.

Table 8.5 *Income tax*

	Tax rate %	1999/2000 band £
Basic rate band	23	28,000
Higher rate band	40	28,000+
Personal allowance (under 65)		4335
Married couple's allowance (restricted to 10%; both under 65)		1970

A particularly popular form of 'perk' is the company car. Here the benefit is measured by reference to scales laid down by the Inland Revenue depending on the list price and age of the car. The benefit is calculated as 35 per cent of the list price of the car when new plus accessories, but less any capital contributions made by the employee. The value of the benefit is reduced by one quarter for cars more than four years old. When the employee uses the car for between 2,500 and 18,000 miles during the tax year the benefit is reduced to 25 per cent of the price and to 15 per cent if the business mileage is over 18,000 in the tax year. An additional charge scale applies where the company petrol is supplied for private use.

Remember that the actual cost to the employee is the tax on these scale charges.

Pensions

Pensions can make all the difference to you, whether you are self-employed or not.

Personal pension schemes came into force on 1 July 1988. These schemes are available to both employees and the self-employed. Unlike their predecessors, i.e. retirement annuities, the employer is able to contribute to personal pensions (known as PPSs). Our couple could normally pay only up to 17.5 per cent of their relevant earnings into a pension scheme, though this can be increased for people more than 35 years old. But the company could pay much higher contributions (subject to Inland Revenue approval) and so reduce the CT charge correspondingly. However, if you are going to start a pension scheme you have got to be sure you want it in addition to finding the cash to pay for it.

Let us look at the finances. Take a man aged 53 with a salary of £15,000 out of his one-man-band company. He wants to retire at 60 with a tax-free lump sum of one and a half times his final salary and a pension thereafter of two-thirds of his final salary or a reduced pension in view of the lump sum. The annual contribution for the next seven or eight years could be as high as £54,000 simply because of the applicant's age. The older you are, the higher the premiums become for the same amount of money.

There are a number of special schemes now and it is advisable to contact your independent insurance consultant to find out the most suitable one for you. Your decision, however, should rest on commercial principles rather than on purely tax considerations.

There is something of a pensions revolution under way and you should make it a priority to find out how it affects you. Telegraph Publications have published a pensions guide which is available through bookshops or directly from the *Daily Telegraph*.

IMPLICATIONS

The different types of taxation dealt with in this chapter must be considered separately and, unless the businessman has a financial background, it would be advisable for him to discuss the implications with his accountant *before* he starts trading. The *Daily Telegraph* publishes a series of tax guides specifically aimed at small businesses, whether or not they are trading as limited companies or are self-employed.

Before the reduction in the level of corporation tax, many companies considered their accounts in the light of how much tax they would have to pay rather than from sound business principles. This has changed and will in all likelihood continue to change. None of us likes paying tax; the small businessman finds it unrewarding to work all hours only to have his hard-earned money taken away by the taxman. If it makes it easier, consider that if you were not earning money you would not be liable for tax.

Further changes were announced for the tax year 2000/2001 in the budget of April 1999. These changes will be addressed in the next edition of this book.

Checklist: Preparing tax

☐ Check with your accountant that the form of your business (ie: sole trader, partnership, unlimited liability or limited liability) is the most tax efficient.

☐ Have you included National Insurance within your tax planning and recruitment costs?

☐ Consider ways to stay below £300,000 profit if you are close to this figure, such as increasing the company pension scheme or taking on additional plant and equipment.

☐ Examine the advantages of registering for VAT, if your annual turnover is under £51,000, such as recovering VAT on expenses

☐ Identify additional record-keeping required for VAT registration.

---

9 Planning for Tax and Using the Incentives

The small business entrepreneur is currently fashionable in government circles, and a number of schemes have been introduced to make life easier for him. A summary at the end of this chapter lists the more recent changes and incentives. This chapter also looks at planning for tax and lists a number of relevant points which need to be taken into consideration. It cannot be stressed too strongly that for sole traders and partnerships consultation with your tax consultant is essential, as no two personal situations are ever the same. The other section in this chapter looks at the effectiveness of some of the government schemes and introduces you to some key questions you ought to be asking yourself, whether as a new business or as an investor. Chapter 8 has already explained the possible benefits and drawbacks of the graduated tax rates, and the dangers of getting caught in the marginal relief band. It has also pointed out the pitfalls for the small company which has not as yet registered for VAT or the dangers of forgetting to do so.

INITIAL COSTS

If you are going to start a new business you will spend money on printing, advertising, legal fees and perhaps rental of an office or factory. The incentive for the small business is that your expenses for up to seven years before you trade will be allowable against tax on commencement, provided that those expenses would have been allowable had you started to trade.

Table 9.1 *Which form of business should I choose?*

	Sole trader/partnership	Company
General	unlimited liability	limited liability (but note possibility of personal guarantees by directors). Also note the stipulations laid out in the Insolvency Act 1986 with regard to directors' liabilities and responsibilities
	statutory audit not required	statutory audit may be required
	annual returns need not be submitted or statutory books kept	annual returns must be submitted and statutory books kept
	no legal continuity on death	legal continuity
	no restrictions on drawings from business	company law in general prohibits loans to directors. Share capital may only be withdrawn: □ in the winding up of the company, or □ where there is a reduction in the company's share capital sanctioned by the courts, or □ where the company buys back its own shares under the arrangements allowed under the Companies Act 1981 and the Finance Act 1982 (see page 160)

Table 9.1 *Continued*

	Sole trader/partnership	Company
Taxation	income tax charged at rates from 10 per cent to 40 per cent depending on profits	corporation tax for small companies 20 per cent. This tax increases as a company grows and depends on profits. At present the top rate is 30 per cent
	'current year' basis from April 1997 (except in opening and closing years of trading)	'actual' basis of assessment
	lower total NI contributions (but fewer benefits)	higher total NI contributions by company as well as directors if employees, but better benefits
	relief for personal pension premiums	relief for personal pension premiums
	single charge to capital gains tax on disposal of assets of assets and subsequent	possible double charge to capital gains tax on disposal withdrawal of capital, e.g. on liquidation
	no capital duty on formation	capital duty payable on formation
	interest relief on money borrowed to invest in business, as capital or as a loan	interest relief to individuals only on money borrowed to invest in company as share capital or by way of a loan

WHICH STRUCTURE IS BEST?

There is no golden rule about which particular form of business structure is best. They all have to be individually examined and applied to your personal circumstances; Table 9.1 summarises the main differences.

The difference between a sole trader and a partnership from a tax point of view is small; whether you are a sole trader or partnership depends on whether you are going into business on your own or with somebody else. The costs of running this sort of operation are considerably less than those incurred when running a company.

The main additional expense of running a company is probably the audit fee. However, limited companies with an annual turnover of less than £350,000 can choose not to have a statutory audit. For all companies, a shareholder can request an audit, regardless of turnover, providing that he holds at least 10 per cent of the shares.

Despite these audit exemptions, the 'true and fair' annual accounts must still be prepared in the existing prescribed format and sent to Companies House nine months after the year end. Many banks are likely to request audited rather than unaudited accounts when they consider overdraft and loan positions, and the audit exemption may not therefore be entirely at the discretion of the shareholders.

On the other hand, as a sole trader or partnership you will certainly need to have accounts prepared to send to the tax inspector and these may well also be required by the bank in the case of a loan or large overdraft; in any case properly prepared accounts must be an important ingredient in the management of your business. The other costs which you can incur in a company that you do not have in a partnership or as a sole trader are those arising out of certain statutory obligations imposed in the running of the company: having meetings, keeping statutory books, sending in the annual return to be registered at Companies House, and so on.

It is also generally easier to draw money, as a direct loan, from a sole trader's business or from a partnership. Let us say you are

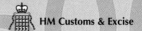
HM Customs & Excise

"taking account of the euro"

It may affect you...

"if you need advice about

accounting or dealing in the

euro, please contact your

local HM Customs & Excise

Advice Centre"

DEALING WITH CUSTOMERS AND SUPPLIERS

PAYMENT OF TAXES AND DUTIES

BUSINESS RECORDS

HM CUSTOMS & EXCISE REQUIREMENTS

The euro may affect you.

please contact
0171 620 1313
for further information

a director of a company. Now it is generally contrary to company law for a director to take money out of a company as a loan, so if you want to draw money out it has got to be by way of salary or bonus. If you take it out in this way you have got to deduct PAYE (Pay As You Earn). With an established sole trader or partnership you can have drawings throughout the year and pay the tax later and in two stages.

As an example, take somebody who is starting in business after being made redundant and who has received a redundancy payment of, say, £20,000. To start a business, he will have to spend, say, £10,000 on capital equipment – plant and machinery, fixtures and fittings. After the first 12 months most businesses might make a loss. However, let us say that he does quite well and comes out even; therefore there is no profit or loss. But he needs to take some money out of the business to live on; let us say he takes £6,000 out.

If it was a company, it would have made a loss of £6,000 because he paid himself a salary of that amount and all he can do is carry it forward and set it off against future profits. He has actually paid some tax – PAYE on the salary of £6,000.

As a sole trader, his drawings of £6,000 do not count as salary; he is just drawing in advance of profits, although he has not made any. All he has done is break even. If, however, he has made a loss in this first period, apart from his drawings, he can carry that loss back for three years into all his previous earnings. In fact, this relief is available for trading losses in the first four years of business. If he paid tax during those years he may therefore be able to recover it up to the level of the losses incurred, provided he is operating as a sole trader or in a partnership. In a company, it would cost him the PAYE and NI on £6,000 which might amount to, say, £950.

An employer has to pay higher NI contributions in respect of his employees, including the directors of his company. It costs a bit more, but the employee receives better benefits out of those contributions. If you are operating as a company you can generally set up better personal pension arrangements than a sole trader or partnership.

The tax rules about converting a sole trader or partnership into a company can be quite complex, particularly regarding the timing of the change.

The partnership will be assessed for each of the first four years on actual profits arising during that period with the previous year's basis operating for the fifth and subsequent year. This rule applies only to established partnerships, not to newly set-up ones.

In practice you may find that large suppliers prefer to do business with a limited company rather than with a sole trader or partnership; therefore some commercial pressure may be brought to bear on the need to incorporate. All these aspects should be kept under constant review in consultation with your accountant.

TAX PLANNING

This subject has never been more important. The progressive reduction of the rates of corporation tax has meant that the deferment of corporation tax liabilities will be a certain means of saving tax. This section does no more than indicate areas which may be worth examining more closely. The operation of the tax system, company law and practice in all these areas is complex and once again it is essential that professional advice is taken when looking at particular situations.

Year-end planning

The planning for the review of a company's tax position should take place well before the year end as part of an ongoing programme involving directors and advisers. Areas for consideration include:

- ☐ Hire purchase; claim capital allowances on full cash price.
- ☐ Lease or buy? Can the business absorb the full capital allowances? How do interest rates compare on a lease contract and bank borrowing?
- ☐ Rent or buy? Again, can the business absorb full capital allowances? Consider the impact of industrial building allowances and the 'machinery' element in buildings.

☐ Are your investments tax efficient? What is the best use of surplus funds?

Salaries and dividends

It used to be accepted that for tax purposes salary was preferable to dividend, but there are further points which need consideration before a decision is made. These are listed below.

☐ Salaries in excess of the justifiable commercial level may be challenged by the Inland Revenue. Not generally a problem except where directors' wives are employed with no real duties.

☐ The aim should be to raise directors' remuneration up to a level where the individual's marginal rate of income tax at least equates to the company's marginal rate of corporation tax. This can be achieved by fixing bonus payments after the year end.

☐ PAYE on remuneration may be due for payment to the Inland Revenue earlier than the company's corporation tax liability. A cash-flow problem may be avoided or reduced by providing for payment of the bonus (as noted in the above point) some time after the balance sheet date. However, remember that PAYE is due when the individual is able to draw down against his bonus entitlement, *not* when he actually does; it is generally accepted practice that if PAYE on a bonus is paid within nine months after a year end, the bonus can be treated as part of that year's expenditure in the accounts.

☐ Impact on NI contributions.

Fringe benefits

Although legislation is much tighter now, scope still exists for providing directors and higher paid employees with various forms of non-cash benefits. There are a number of points to remember, not least of which is the wide definition of the word 'director'.

Earnings thresholds for employees earning over £8,500 per annum include:

- [ ] all salaries as generally understood;
- [ ] value of all benefits received;
- [ ] all expenses reimbursed before any allowable deductions.

Various perks also have a measure of taxable benefit, such as living accommodation and company cars.

Pension schemes

Although at present pension schemes offer the best opportunity for tax planning which will benefit both the company and its employees in all categories, currently the main advantages of an approved occupational pension scheme are the substantial tax reliefs and exemptions that are allowed, particularly in the payment of tax-free lump sums on retirement or on death in service.

Purchase of own shares

Under the 1981 Companies Act, companies were given the power to purchase their own shares. Under the 1982 Finance Act, tax relief was introduced to enable unquoted trading companies to make such purchases without undue cost in terms of tax. This means that the shareholder who is selling his shares can treat the sale as a normal capital gains tax disposal, with no tax charges payable by the company. Where relief does not apply, cash passing from company to shareholder must be treated as an income distribution, with advanced corporation tax payable by the company, and possibly a higher rate liability on the shareholder.

There are a number of stringent requirements that have to be satisfied, but this is a route that may well be worth examining when an investor in the company wishes to realise some or all of his investment and there is no market readily available.

WHAT TYPE OF CAPITAL IS BEST?

Whether you use bank money or not depends on whether you can get it from the bank. If you have the money to put in the business yourself, and if you can make a good profit, why give some of it to the bank? You may feel you need extra money. While under-capitalising is a mistake, at the same time you may not wish to get tied up with interest payments on borrowed money. On the other hand, you may prefer to keep at least some of your personal capital outside the business in case of emergency.

The question of how much money you should put into the business by way of share capital (in the case of a company) and by way of a loan – in other words, your own money, not outside finance – should be decided on commercial factors. It is something which you will need to go into with your advisers at the time. A guideline is that you ought to have sufficient share capital invested to make the company look a reasonably substantial operation. Table 9.2 sets out the options.

BENEFITS FOR THE INVESTOR

Benefits for the investor:

- ☐ Tax relief can be claimed on the money borrowed to put into a company or partnership, provided the borrower is active in the management of the business.
- ☐ If unquoted companies in which you have invested lose money, you can set your loss off against your other income.
- ☐ Where a tax loss arises in either the tax year of commencement or any of the following three years, the loss can be set against the taxpayer's total income for the three previous years (relief is given for the earliest available year first). In certain circumstances, therefore, relief for a trading loss will be given in a tax year before the trade commenced.

LEGISLATION DESIGNED TO EASE THE TAX BURDEN

- [ ] Corporation tax for small companies is 20 per cent if taxable profits do not exceed £300,000. Marginal relief at 32.5 per cent applies if taxable profits are between £300,000 and £1,500,000. Profits exceeding £1,500,000 are taxed at 30 per cent.
- [ ] VAT registration is only required if taxable supplies exceed £51,000 or if there are grounds for believing that the value of taxable supplies made in the next 30 days will exceed £51,000.
- [ ] A business raising self-billed invoices will be responsible for establishing the precise VAT liability.

LEGISLATION DESIGNED TO ENCOURAGE INVESTMENT IN SMALL COMPANIES

Relief for certain pre-trading expenses

Expenditure of a revenue nature which is incurred before trading begins is eligible for relief:

- [ ] if it is incurred within seven years if trading starts after 5 April 1995 (five years if trading begins before 5 April 1995); and if
- [ ] it would have been allowed as a deduction for tax purposes if it had been incurred after trading had begun.

Examples of pre-trading expenses which are eligible for relief include rent, rates and employees' wages.

Table 9.2 *Share capital or loan capital?*

	Share capital	Loan capital
Tax relief on payment of dividends/interest	No, but ACT may be credited against the company's CT liability	Yes
Voting rights and a say in the running of the company	Yes	No
Right to participate in profits	Yes	No
Receipts of dividends/interest taxable	Yes	Yes
Can be issued at a discount	No	Yes
Dividend/interest payable if the company is making a loss	No	Yes
Easy to reduce share/loan capital not paid	No	Yes
Tax relief if share/loan capital not paid	Yes	Yes/No

Relief for interest paid on money borrowed for investment

1. Interest relief on borrowing to invest in close companies: an individual has to satisfy one of two conditions before he may be able to obtain any tax relief for interest on funds borrowed in order to invest in or lend to a close company. These are:

- ☐ he must have a material interest in the company (i.e. greater than 5 per cent of the ordinary share capital); or
- ☐ he must work for the greater part of his time for the company or an associated company and hold some shares in the company.

2. Interest relief on borrowing to invest in employee-controlled companies: where shares in a company are acquired by its employees so that they obtain control of the company (e.g. an employee buy-out), an individual who borrows money to fund his purchase of shares may be able to obtain tax relief on the interest paid, subject to various conditions being satisfied.
3. Interest relief on borrowing to invest in partnerships: provided that he is a member of the partnership, an individual who borrows money to invest in a partnership, either as capital or as loan, or to buy an interest in the partnership from another partner, e.g. one who is retiring, may be able to obtain tax relief on the interest paid.

Income tax relief for capital losses on shares in unquoted trading companies

An individual, subject to certain conditions, may set against his taxable income a capital loss arising on the disposal of shares in an unquoted trading company. This relief does *not* normally apply to the loss of money *lent to the company.*

A claim for the relief may be made for the year immediately following and must be made within two years of the end of the year for which the relief is claimed. Any unused balance of the loss will be available to set against earned income and then against unearned income.

The Enterprise Investment Scheme

The Enterprise Investment Scheme is discussed in Chapter 12 However, it is worth mentioning that for investments that qualify, an investor is able to claim tax relief at the lower rate (currently 20 per cent) of income tax. The amount invested in the tax year, up to a maximum of £150,000 each tax year, can be set against income for that year, with a potential tax saving of £30,000 for the investor. Capital gains tax relief also applies. If sold at a profit, the capital gain is exempt from tax. If sold at a loss, or if the company ceases trading for genuine commercial reasons, the capital loss less the income tax relief already received on the investment can be set against income for the year or set against any capital gain in the usual way. The shares must be held for five years to qualify for all the reliefs.

Relief for costs of raising business loan finance

Expenditure which has been incurred on the incidental costs of either obtaining or repaying qualifying loan finance is allowed as a deduction in computing the trading profits of a business for tax purposes, or, if appropriate, as a management expense for investment companies. For this purpose incidental costs include, among others, fees, commissions, advertising and printing.

In this connection a qualifying loan is defined as being any borrowing which meets either of the following conditions:

- [ ] the interest on the loan is deductible in computing the trading profits of the business (e.g. bank loan); or
- [ ] the interest on the loan is treated as a charge on income (e.g. loans from institutions to finance trading).

The relief is extended to the incidental costs of raising convertible loans, provided that the conversion date of such loans is not earlier than three years from the issue of the loan. Any abortive costs of obtaining finance are also deductible if the finance would have been a qualifying loan.

Checklist: Planning for tax incentives

☐ Discuss the relative merits of the different forms of business for your personal circumstances with your accountant.

☐ Schedule in the review of your tax position well before the year-end to consider all areas that affect tax liability.

☐ Examine the pros and cons of paying dividends or salaries.

☐ Identify non-cash benefits for directors and higher paid employees.

☐ Discuss with your adviser how much personal capital should be put into your business.

☐ Consider if your local Enterprise Zone can offer benefits and contact the Department of Environment, Transport and the Regions for details.

☐ Consider whether you qualify for interest relief on investment borrowing.

☐ Examine the details of the Enterprise Investment Scheme if you want to encourage investors.

10 Recruitment and Employment Law

Employment law is changing all the time. Many of the changes come about as a result of decisions of the European Court and involve new rights for your employees and new obligations for you as an employer. Important recent examples are the new rules which limit working time and give workers the right to paid leave. This chapter explains some of the main rules and also tells you where you can obtain more detailed advice.

TAKING ON STAFF

There are certain elements that you must be absolutely sure about before you recruit.

☐ Ask yourself whether you need another member of staff.
☐ Write a full job description listing tasks in order of importance. Be specific and take into account the relationship of the job to other tasks being carried out in the work environment.
☐ When advertising the vacancy select the appropriate media for the job. Make sure that the job title and description are clearly shown and that you can stand by your printed word.
☐ Shop around for a recruitment agency as fees can vary from 5 per cent to as high as 22 per cent. Make sure that you know the agency's terms and whether advertising costs are covered in the bill. Provide the agency with a job specification,

the type of person you are looking for and the qualifications that the candidate must have. Local job centres provide candidates for general appointments.

Discrimination

You must not discriminate, personally or through the agency, on grounds of race, sex or marital status. Job requirements and selection criteria must not be indirectly discriminatory in any of these ways, unless they are job related and can be objectively justified.

There is now no limit on the compensation which you could be ordered to pay if you discriminate unlawfully against job applicants or employees. Leaflets and information can be obtained from the Equal Opportunities Commission (0161–833 9244) or the Commission for Racial Equality (0171–828 7022).

There must also be no discrimination on grounds of trade union membership or non-membership.

There is also a law, the Disability Discrimination Act 1995, to prevent unjustified discrimination against disabled job applicants and employees. Employers can also be required to adjust their premises, equipment and businesses to change features or arrangements which place the disabled at a disadvantage. The employment provisions will apply to you if you have 15 or more employees.

You are legally required to check that new employees are entitled to work and remain in Great Britain. If the worker does not have a National Insurance number, you will need to see some other documentary evidence of work status, such as a work permit, UK birth certificate or European Union passport. You should take and keep a copy of the document which is produced to you. You must not act in a discriminatory way, for example by assuming from the colour of the worker's skin that the worker is or is not entitled to work in Great Britain.

Application forms

Whether or not you are using an agency to recruit applicants, always make sure that you have a proper application form to be

Reducing risk!

Starting a business from scratch is both exciting and incredibly daunting, especially when you consider that over 80% of 'start-ups' fail. All of the blood sweat and tears, not to mention the hard-earned savings that have been invested are lost.

There has to be a better way!

Whilst there is not a guaranteed route to success (or else everyone would be working for themselves), there are business vehicles that can be used to substantially reduce the risk. The most successful of which is franchising.

However, there is a price to pay for that safety blanket. The Franchisor will charge an up-front Franchise Fee that should cover the cost of training but NOT be a contributor to profit and, on an ongoing basis, a Management Services Fee that pays for the constant support and the use of the brand name and methodology.

Look for a Franchisor that has a strong brand name and a highly efficient and proven training and support programme. The higher the fee, the more in-depth and comprehensive the training should be. A lower up-front fee does not mean better value, but potentially a higher risk of failure because the Franchisor has less capital to invest back into your business.

You should also find an industry that you enjoy – why invest time and money to build your own business when you resent going to work and you are unhappy?

Making a profit is important, but so too are the intellectual rewards – the two must be balanced.

Humana International Group, an MRI company, is not only the world's largest search organisation, it is also 100% franchised. The Humana International Group recently expanded its global search and recruitment capabilities as a result of its acquisition by Management Recruiters International (MRI) in April of 1999. Already the largest company of its kind in the world with over 800 offices, the MRI network now approaches 1000 offices on six continents. Systemwide billings for MRI/Humana are projected to exceed USD$600 million in 1999.

Humana trains successful executives to parlay their accumulated business experience back into the industries they understand best, and by doing so add significant value to their clients. Humana delivers the best people available to their clients and charges a professional fee for doing so.

The Executive's Choice

HUMANA INTERNATIONAL

SPECIALISTS IN SEARCH

Last year our Franchisees invoiced over £18 million in professional fees on a global basis.

Use your contacts, acumen and leadership to build your own executive recruitment business with our proven training and support.

Contact Kevin Cox, on **01753 740 020**

BRITISH FRANCHISE ASSOCIATION FULL MEMBER

THE HUMANA INTERNATIONAL GROUP PLC,
HUMANA HOUSE, 11 ETON HIGH STREET, ETON,
BERKSHIRE SL4 6AT   FAX: 01753 842 428
E-Mail: KCox@Humana-Intl.com
Website: http://www.Humana-Intl.com

HUMANA INTERNATIONAL GROUP
PLC
SPECIALISTS IN SEARCH

completed by all candidates. If you are using an agency insist that they submit copies of application forms for all candidates put forward for interview. These forms are valuable documents because they form the basis of staff records, and must be filed away in a private location with strictly limited access. As soon as anyone replies to your advertisement, he should be sent an application form. If it is properly designed, it should have space for you to make notes during an interview. Notes are essential so that you can, if necessary, show subsequently that you are recruiting for the job on capability alone and that you are not exercising discrimination. If you do not do this, it would be very difficult to prove at a later date that you have not discriminated in filling the vacancy. You need the evidence of your thoughts at the time to show that you assessed the person in the light of the requirements of the job.

Before each interview read through the completed forms and make a note of any questions you need answers to, or any clarification which is required. If you find that a job applicant is disabled, you must consider and discuss ways of overcoming any problems which this causes (including changes to the job itself). You must also consider whether any special interview arrangements are called for in order to overcome or mitigate the effects of the disability. Rejecting a job applicant because of a disability (or for any related reason, such as difficulties with wheelchair access) is lawful only if it is an unavoidable last resort.

Making an offer

When you offer employment, do so in writing. Make it clear in your letter whether the offer is conditional on satisfactory references, a medical, signature of a formal contract or a trial period. If you make an unconditional offer which is accepted you cannot then make it conditional on any of these matters.

There is no need for a formal contract of employment. The offer letter and the employee's written acceptance can constitute a contract. It is important to spell out the main terms of the employment in the offer letter, including the duration of the contract, if it is to be for a fixed term, or the length of notice which the employee is required to give and entitled to receive.

It is risky to commit yourself to a fixed term contract or lengthy notice period. If the employee proves to be unsatisfactory, this will not generally entitle you to terminate the contract without the risk of having to pay the employee for the full contract or notice period.

You will need to have a contract drawn up by a solicitor if you wish to impose restrictions on what the employee can do after the employment ends. The general rule is that a former employee can set up in competition and poach your customers unless there are enforceable restrictions in the employment contract. You will need detailed advice on any restrictions, because they are unenforceable if unreasonably stringent.

Certain terms of the contract, if not contained in an employment contract, must be notified in writing to the employee within two months after commencement. You will be able to obtain a leaflet from an Employment Office with full details of these.

One of the matters to be specified is the date when the period of continuous employment began. This will usually be the date when the employment with you commenced. However if you acquire a business with existing employees they will automatically become your employees under their existing contract terms. Their continuous employment then runs from the date when their original employment began. This is the effect of the Transfer of Undertakings (Protection of Employment) Regulations (TUPE).

Any change to the statutory particulars must be notified in writing to the employee within one month.

Health and safety

It is a mistake to think of health and safety legislation only in terms of factory accidents, caused by dangerous machinery or fork-lift trucks. Accidents and damage to health also occur in shops and offices. They can be caused, for example, by faulty wiring, unsafe equipment or badly designed office furniture.

As an employer you have a responsibility to provide a safe and healthy working environment. If you have at least five employees you must also have a written statement of your general health and

SW+H Health & Safety Ltd was formed in 1995 to provide Health & Safety services and advice to small businesses in London and Southern England. We are a young, small company, understand the problems involved in setting up a new business.

Our initial consultation is important in determining our client's requirements and is free of charge. We try to be as practical and as approachable as possible and tailor our advice to suit the precise needs of a particular client.

Our initial task in usually to prepare a simple Health & Safety policy for a new business to ensure that it complies with the Law; however, as our client's business grows so can our services. These can include the preparation of risk assessments and written procedures or indeed the setting up of a comprehensive Health & Safety Management system complying with recognised British Standards.

Continuing commitment to our clients is important and we operate a telephone *"Help Line"* providing advice and guidance on Health, Safety and Environmental matters.

safety policy and the arrangements for carrying out the policy. Many guidance notes, leaflets and codes of practice are available from the Health and Safety Executive (HSE) (some of them free of charge). You can obtain information and advice from the HSE Information Centre, Broad Lane, Sheffield S3 7HQ or by telephoning a different office on 0541 545500.

You must also carry out all necessary precautions against fire. Guidance on fire precautions is continued in several official publications which you can buy from the Stationery Office. You will need a Fire Certificate if more than 20 persons are employed in total on your premises (or more than 10 persons elsewhere than on the ground floor).

You could face claims from fellow employees or third parties if one of your employees, acting in the course of his employment, causes injury or damage. You must take out employer and public liability insurance cover in respect of your premises and all your business activities. You must also ensure that the appropriate cover for business use is in force whenever cars or other vehicles are being used for the purposes of your business.

The Working Time regulations have been in force since 1 October 1998. They give a wide range of rights to employees and other workers including, for the first time, a statutory right to paid leave. This right arises after 13 weeks of continuous working or employment. The minimum annual paid leave is three weeks (rising to four weeks with effect from 23 November 1999). Working time (including overtime) must be recorded and must not exceed an average of 48 hours (averaged over a period which is usually 17 weeks) unless the worker has signed a written agreement opting out of this restriction. There are further provisions restricting the hours of night workers. Night workers have the right to free health assessments. The regulations also give workers rights to rest breaks and daily and weekly rest periods.

Discrimination and equal pay

The laws against racial, sex and marriage discrimination apply not only to recruitment and dismissal but also to the way in which you treat your existing staff. Decisions on such matters as promotion, training, fringe benefits, allocation of work and warnings and other disciplinary matters must not be influenced by the race, sex or marital status of the employee. If you have 15 or more employees, the new Disability Discrimination Act gives rights to any who are disabled. You can obtain from HMSO a *Code of Practice*, £9.95, ISBN 0 11 270954 0, and also *Guidance on the Definition of Disability*, £7.50, ISBN 0 11 270955 9.

It is particularly important that you should take steps to prevent any sexual or racial harassment. A good starting point is to make it clear to all your employees that harassment of fellow employees or customers will be treated as serious misconduct and could lead to summary dismissal. Unless you take effective measures, you could be held responsible for harassment or other acts of discrimination by one of your employees, even though you had not authorised these acts.

The general principle in relation to equal pay is that if you have employees of different sexes doing similar work, or work of equal value, then they should each receive the same rate of pay. They should also each enjoy the same contract terms in all other respects. If there is to be any differential in pay or difference in other contract terms, then there must be some good reason for it, unrelated to the difference in sex. For example you may legitimately pay a woman more than a man, even though they are doing similar work, if she is more highly qualified or has longer service or greater experience.

Maternity rights

Pregnant employees have the following rights:

- ☐ time off for ante-natal care;
- ☐ protection against dismissal;
- ☐ statutory maternity pay (SMP);
- ☐ maternity leave.

You must not dismiss an employee because she is pregnant or because she has been off work with a pregnancy related illness. If it is unsafe for a pregnant employee to continue to do her job (for example, because it involves heavy lifting) you must find her suitable alternative work, or, if none is available, suspend her on full pay.

Every expectant mother has the right to take maternity leave of up to 14 weeks and to return to work at the end of that period. During this maternity leave period, the employee is entitled to retain all her contractual benefits other than pay (eg use of a company car if you provide one under the terms of her contract).

The 14 week period for maternity leave is shortly to be increased to 18 weeks, to match the period for which SMP is payable.

There is a right to a much longer period of leave (but without SMP beyond the 18 weeks and without a continued right to contractual benefits unless you have agreed to provide them) if the employee has worked for you two years up to the beginning of the 11th week before that in which the baby is due. An employee taking this additional leave must comply with various notice provisions and must generally return to work within 29 weeks from the start of the week in which the actual confinement falls. The qualifying period of two years is shortly to be reduced to one year.

If an employee is unable through illness to present herself for work after her maternity leave (whether the standard leave or extended leave), you cannot treat her employment as automatically terminated.

This is a summary of employee rights. For detailed rules and regulations, you should obtain a leaflet from your local Employment Office.

Before the end of 1999, there are to be new laws giving parents and adoptive parents of both sexes the right to take unpaid leave of up to three months (probably spread over two or more periods of leave) following the birth or adoption of each child. There will also be a right to take a reasonable amount of time off to deal with family emergencies.

Sickness absences

Your employees will generally be entitled to statutory sick pay (SSP) for the first 28 weeks of any sickness absence (except the first three days) but there are special provisions where there are two or more absences with short gaps between them. You will be able to set the SSP paid in any month against your National Insurance contributions to the extent that the amount of the SSP paid in the month exceeds 13 per cent of your contributions payable for the month. You are required to keep detailed records and you should obtain a leaflet from an Employment Office for full details of the scheme.

Some employers operate contractual or discretionary arrangements which are more favourable than the SSP scheme (e.g. full pay for absences of up to six months in any calendar year). You cannot, however, impose a scheme which is less favourable to your employees than the SSP scheme.

Working with trade unions

At the time of writing, it is up to each employer to decide whether to recognise a trade union. A new law is expected to come into force in the summer of 1999, under which employers may be obliged to grant recognition if a majority of the relevant group of employees belongs to the particular union or if a sufficient majority vote in favour of recognition. This law will not, however, apply to any employees who (taking into account any associated employers) have 20 or fewer employees.

Whether you recognize a union or not, you are required by law to consult representatives of your employees if there are proposals for the transfer of your business or if you have redundancy proposals affecting 20 or more employees at one establishment.

ENDING EMPLOYMENT

There are three essential rules. The first is that you may not dismiss an employee on grounds of race, sex, marital status, disability, pregnancy, trade union membership or non-membership or legitimate trade union activities. The forbidden grounds now also include various kinds of victimisation, such as dismissal for asserting certain statutory rights (e.g. under the Wages Act) or for steps taken in relation to health and safety (e.g. as a health and safety officer). If you dismiss on any of these grounds, you may have to pay very substantial compensation, even if the employee has been with you for only a very short time.

Secondly, you must give the minimum period of notice required under the terms of your contract with the employee. If the contract is silent on the point, the employee may be able to argue that there is an implied right to a lengthy notice period (possibly six months in the case of a senior employee). There is also a statutory minimum notice which you must give to the employee. This period is one week after the employee has been with you for four weeks, rising to one week for each full year of continuous employment up to twelve years.

Thirdly, most employees (whether full-time or part-time) have the right not to be unfairly dismissed. The general rule is that this right does not arise until the employee has been continuously employed for a qualifying period, but there are several exceptions to this general rule (such as dismissal because of pregnancy or trade union membership or non-membership). The qualifying period, at the time of writing, is two years. This period is under challenge in a case being fought in the European Court of Justice. Whatever the outcome of that case, the Government has announced its intention to reduce the qualifying period to one year in 1999. The limit on the compensation which can be awarded for unfair dismissal is also to be raised. The main head of compensation is currently limited to £12,000 but that figure is to be increased to £50,000.

Unfair dismissal

There are two hurdles which you have to overcome in order to defeat an unfair dismissal claim. The first is to show that the dismissal was for a substantial reason justifying the dismissal of the employee. The most common are misconduct, incapacity or redundancy. Incapacity can include long-term or regular sickness absences as well as incompetence.

You must never dismiss an employee for an absence caused by a pregnancy related illness. You will also need to take legal and medical advice before considering dismissal for absences caused wholly or partly by disability.

Secondly, you must act reasonably both in deciding to dismiss the employee and in the way in which you go about the matter. For example it would generally be unreasonable to dismiss an employee for incompetence unless the employee has been given a genuine chance to improve; or for a minor offence of misconduct (such as lateness) unless there is a current final warning; or for redundancy unless you have fully considered all possibilities of alternative work.

The golden rule is that, whatever the reason for dismissal, the employee is entitled to a hearing before a final decision to dismiss is taken. In the case of misconduct dismissals, this involves a disciplinary hearing at which the employee has had full details of the allegations (and sight of any statements) and is given a full opportunity to respond to them.

A decision to dismiss should be made only after careful deliberation and discussion. It is *never* appropriate to make a snap decision. If you believe that you have conclusive evidence that an employee has been stealing from you, you must *not* sack the employee on the spot. You should suspend the employee on full pay and arrange a disciplinary hearing.

It is always prudent to take advice before dismissing an employee. Some possible sources of advice are mentioned below.

Redundancy

An employee who is made redundant after at least two years' continuous service is entitled to a redundancy payment. The amount varies according to age, pay and length of service. For example, an employee aged 35, with gross pay of more than £220 per week and 10 years' continuous service, would be entitled to £2,200. You may not need to make a redundancy payment, if you offer suitable alternative work and the employee refuses unreasonably.

A redundancy dismissal could also be an unfair dismissal if you have unreasonable selection criteria or if you apply them unreasonably. Common mistakes are failure to consult the employee before a final decision is made and failure to consider the possibility of alternative employment. You must not select an employee for redundancy because she is pregnant or on maternity leave. Redundancy selection must not be influenced by considerations of race, sex, marital status, disability or trade union membership or non-membership or activities.

Constructive dismissal

Sometimes you may stumble into a dismissal without intending to do so. If you break an express or implied term of the employment contract, your employee may be entitled to walk out and claim to have been dismissed.

A common example of a constructive dismissal is the case where the employer imposes a pay cut or a demotion in breach of the employee's contract. If you have a business need to vary any employee's terms of employment, then you should take advice on how to achieve this variation.

GETTING HELP

The matters on which you are most likely to need expert advice include preparing an employment contract, varying important contract terms, responding to complaints of discrimination, complying with Working Time Regulations, handling redundancies and other dismissals and dealing with Employment Tribunal claims against you. You may be able to obtain legal advice through an employers' or trade association to which you belong. Otherwise you should go to a solicitor who is experienced in dealing with employment law. You may be able to obtain recommendations from other employers who are known to you or from your other professional advisers.

The Advisory Conciliation and Arbitration Service (ACAS) is an important source of free advice for employers who are considering a dismissal or who have some other employment problem. ACAS has public inquiry points at its regional offices throughout the country. There are also important ACAS publications, such as the code of practice on disciplinary practice and procedures. There are currently public inquiry points in the following towns and cities:

Birmingham	0121 622 5050	Liverpool	0151 427 8881
Bristol	0117 974 4066	London	0171 396 5100
Cardiff	01222 762636	Manchester	0161 228 3222
Fleet	01252 811868	Newcastle	0191 261 2191
Glasgow	0141 204 2677	Nottingham	0115 969 3355
Leeds	0113 243 1371		

ACAS also play an important role in achieving settlements in unfair dismissal and other Employment Tribunal cases and disputes. The general rule is that you can achieve a binding settlement only by means of a compromise agreement, on which the employee must be advised by a solicitor, or through ACAS.

DISCUSS PROBLEMS

Much of employment law is technical and complicated. The laws relating to equal pay, maternity rights and TUPE are particularly difficult.

You should be able to avoid most major problems, however, if you manage your business efficiently and treat your employees as human beings. Discuss problems with your employees, make or confirm agreements in writing, base your decisions on a reasoned approach rather than instinct or prejudice, record all your major decisions and the reasons for them, take time to reflect on key decisions and keep all relevant documents in your personnel files. If you do all these things you should not go far wrong.

Checklist: Planning for recruitment

☐ Have you analysed the jobs you will offer?
☐ Is there an adequate labour force available?
☐ Have you contacted the job centre concerning staff regulations?
☐ Will you offer training? If so, have you a training plan?
☐ Have you prepared or purchased specimen contracts of employment?
☐ What pay, holidays, sickness, hours of service etc will you allow and do you comply with the Working Time Regulations?*
☐ Have you considered staff rest and hygiene facilities?
☐ If you employ over 15 staff have you adjusted your premises and equipment to comply with the Disability Discrimination Act?*
☐ What else should be considered in your case?

*added to original material from *Running you own Business* DfEE

---

11 | **Starting Off in Export**

BEFORE YOU START

The need to take export seriously is today more important than ever because we now live in a Single European Market, which now has a single currency for the conduct of trade with 11 of its 15 member countries. Even as a small business you cannot escape the implications of living in a single market, because competitors from other European Union (EU) countries are able to compete for your customers here in Britain. Your best defence is probably to compete with them in their own nations. You may, if you prefer, think of this as extending your domestic business and not as exporting. Indeed this would be more forward-thinking than considering other EU countries as export markets. Even so, dealing with customers elsewhere in Europe will inevitably involve you to a considerable degree in export procedures.

While you may be more or less forced to 'export', you need take this no further than Western Europe. However, you may well feel that if you can handle business from other countries in Europe, you could equally well handle it from countries outside Europe. But whatever you do, your aim should be to do profitable business, otherwise it will not be worth having, and, moreover, will almost certainly fail. But bear in mind you must not try to go too fast, or take on too much, while you must certainly limit the amount of any money you may need to borrow.

Look at your company

Before beginning to export it is best to take a good look at your own company and its business. If you have any doubts have a word with your nearest government export assistance office, and see if specialist consultancy help would be beneficial in areas such as marketing, design, manufacturing systems, business planning and financial and information systems. This will ensure that your business is soundly based before you go ahead and expand into export. In England you should ring your local Business Link office, in Scotland, the Scottish Trade International Service, in Wales, the export section of the Welsh Office and in Northern Ireland, the Industrial Development Board for Northern Ireland.

Next, have a word with your accountant, and discuss what you are thinking of doing; in particular, talk about the costs of the project you have in mind, and the facilities you may need. Then talk to your bank, and discuss the figures you showed to your accountant. Make sure the facilities you may require will be available, and for how long.

The DTI publishes a range of useful booklets on exporting and export markets through its 'Business in Europe' service, which gives information and advice on documentation, trade fairs, credit insurance, choosing representatives, and many other aspects of export. The first thing to do is ring the Business in Europe Hotline on 01272 444 888, which is open 24 hours a day, seven days a week, and ask for details of government services in the areas in which you have an interest.

Gather information

Another source of information about exporting is the Association of British Chambers of Commerce, which operates an export marketing research scheme. Moreover, your own Chamber of Commerce may well have an Export Development Adviser (EDA), whose job it is to help a small company devise a coherent and practical plan for export. Your initial consultation is free, and at this stage you will only need that initial guidance, but any further help has to be paid for.

If you still need some reassurance, remember that more and more buyers in the world are demanding specialised goods and services, instead of mass-produced goods and services from enormous multinational companies. As a small business you can take quick action to exploit unexpected opportunities because you do not have the cumbersome procedures which seem obligatory in larger companies. You may be able to avoid the effects of a slump in your domestic trade if you have export business since not all countries experience slumps at the same time. Exporting is exciting, and a welcome change from the rather more prosaic round of domestic business which you will have probably been engaged in for some time.

At this stage, however, you need only decide whether you will or will not start off in export. How and where you do this cannot yet be decided, nor can the extent to which selling overseas will affect your business. There is a good deal more to examine before you have to come to those decisions.

EXPORT MARKET RESEARCH

You may well be advised to start your strategic planning for export by carrying out export market research. This suggestion should be treated with caution because not only does research cost time and money, but it fails to generate business immediately. Moreover, it will not tell you what to do, but merely help you to make up your mind.

What you need to know

Even so, some research will be necessary, but it should be kept to an absolute minimum, and you should obtain as much information as you can for free. Most of what you will need for starting up in export is known as secondary information, i.e. information that has been published. Primary information, which you must obtain yourself, is unlikely to be needed in the initial stages.

The areas you will have to check by research are:

1. The local conditions of any area to which you propose to export. For example, you cannot hope to sell to people in Hong Kong unless you know something about the Chinese

people there, their methods of buying, their needs and wants, etc.

2. You will need to make sure that what you sell, whether goods, services or know-how, is suitable for your prospective customers. For example, it is difficult to sell a milk jug to French women who drink their tea with lemon or their coffee black. Nor can you expect to sell food labelled in English to Dubai.

3. You must understand how goods can be made available to their final users. For instance, you must appreciate the part played by street vendors of household goods in places like Nigeria and Turkey.

4. You should be familiar with the various aspects of physical distribution, i.e. getting your goods delivered overseas. If you sell to Cyprus do you send the goods by sea or air? What documents will be needed, and how do you obtain them? And just as important, how do you get paid by your customers, and how long does this take?

5. If you are going to trade profitably, you must establish your costs and then arrive at prices that are acceptable to your customers, in order to obtain a reasonable contribution to your revenue and a worthwhile return on the capital employed. If you are selling in, say, Saudi Arabia how do you negotiate with the Arab traders, who know only too well how to drive a hard bargain?

Some sources of information

A range of government services are on offer, which are aimed specifically at helping small companies to obtain the essential information they need to start off in export. Details of these can be obtained from the previously mentioned government offices (the telephone number will be in your local directory).

Chambers of Commerce have a great deal of information readily available. Moreover, they have introduced an export marketing research scheme, whereby if a company wants specialised information they will contribute towards the cost of having this obtained locally. Because you will wish to visit places where you are trying to start selling, aim to do this travelling cheaply. One option is to join an Outward Trade Mission, sponsored by a Chamber of Commerce. You cannot take advantage of their help for countries in Europe, but elsewhere you can save most of the travelling costs since these will be paid for you. Moreover, you will meet many people on these missions who can be invaluable to you, and this is particularly important when you are visiting an unfamiliar place.

The problem with information is that there is almost too much of it. So do not become bogged down by market research; only try to find out what you really need to know. A useful publication is *Croner's Reference Book for Exporters*, because it provides a mass of useful facts about countries in addition to the documents needed, transport facilities, etc. Also obtain for any country in which you are interested a copy of the *Hints for Exporters Visiting ...* booklet, published by the Overseas Trades Services (OTS). The books are written by the commercial officers of the British Embassies and High Commissions overseas and are excellent small summaries of local conditions.

Finally, you should start some simple system in your office for collecting any interesting information you come across in your daily life about people and places overseas. It is amazing how quickly this becomes an invaluable source of information, and at little or no cost to the company.

WHERE TO EXPORT

There are, of course, several criteria for choosing where to start trying to sell, the main one being that you should find an area containing customers who are as much like your domestic customers as possible. After all, if you can sell to these people at home then you should also be able to sell to them overseas. In practice it will probably be very difficult to find an identical market, but the closer you can get the better.

Which countries to exclude

You could start by eliminating all those parts of the world where import restrictions or a lack of foreign currency more or less prevent importers buying from you. These are the areas you can best deal with by licensing, and may well include some Eastern European countries and places like Burma, as well as most countries in Central and South America.

Exporting to Europe

Alternatively, you could start in the European Union, because not only does it take over 70 per cent of all British exports, but there are no customs duties payable on EU-originated goods. So, for example, British goods sent to Italy pay no duty, although VAT or its equivalent is payable in all European countries, albeit at different rates. Outside Europe, many regulations affect what you may sell in particular countries, and these regulations may require you to choose some areas in preference to others.

Research your market

Before finally choosing where to start examine the exports of British goods in your field as set out in the _Statistics of Exports_ published by the Government Statistical Office. You can see these figures in the DTI's Export Intelligence Library or any Chamber of Commerce; they will show you where there is business, since if others can trade there you can probably do so too.

Dismiss any parts of the world where you feel there are severe transport problems and decide on where you would feel happiest doing business. Have you perhaps received some approaches in the past which you have not followed up? Or have you relations and friends who could help?

Areas of Western Europe

If you are going to tackle Western Europe, try to think in terms of areas rather than countries. For example, you will find that customers in the north-western part of Germany have much in common with those in Holland and the north of Belgium, where Flemish is spoken, but both German and Dutch are understood.

Another area in northern Europe which is easy enough to reach from the UK is north-eastern France, the south of Belgium, where French is spoken, and the western half of Switzerland. But if you prefer a more Latin market, why not look at the east of Spain, the south of France, the north of Italy and the south of Switzerland – where Italian is spoken.

What you are looking for are groups of compatible customers to whom you can sell. For example, one small company concentrated on Embassy and High Commission staff all over the world, because they have virtually no foreign exchange problems, or customs duties to pay, and found their exports grew rapidly in several countries; another small company began in Portugal because the Chairman had a Portuguese wife. So there are endless reasons why small companies start in different parts of the world; you should choose carefully where to start but be prepared to change if sales do not materialise.

WHAT TO EXPORT

There are three main choices: goods, services and know-how. Taking the last one first, as a small company you may well have valuable assets in the way of a patented process or a good trade mark and name which you can sell overseas by means of some licensing arrangement.

Licensing

The great advantage of licensing for a small company is that you do not have to extend your factory to produce more goods to earn foreign exchange. Moreover, you do not have to be concerned with shipping the goods overseas, arranging their documentation and then worrying about how you will be paid for them. And there are a great many parts of the world where licences to manufacture and sell are eagerly sought, such as Eastern Europe and Central and South America. Hence you export with the minimum of effort, and cash an asset you probably did not realise you possessed.

Export of services

If you sell services remember that a great deal of our foreign currency comes from what are called invisible earnings, i.e. services of various kinds, like banking, insurance, education, design, engineering, etc. If you are a professional selling personal services you can earn commissions from other countries. For example, UK companies specialising in the disposal of waste have secured contracts in the Middle East because local people do not like to be associated with that kind of work.

Where major projects are concerned, such as the building of a hospital or school, or new roads or an airport, these days the originator will demand a package deal so that he can deal with one person and not a whole host of suppliers. Such deals are handled by what are called consortia, and you can as a professional person or company join such consortia, and benefit from the major contracts they handle; for example, an architect may be involved with the building of several hotels in the Caribbean on this basis. Hence a road haulage contractor, for example, is able to seek business wherever he likes, and no longer be restricted in the return loads he carries from outside Britain. Services can be offered under the competition policy of the EU wherever you choose. We have seen the growth of estate agency services on a joint basis between UK companies and those in northern and southern Europe, as people buy a second home or go to live and work in other parts of Europe.

Goods needing modification

When you export goods you may well have to modify or alter them according to local regulations or local customer preferences. Many countries do impose regulations on the exact specifications of goods sold, and these regulations have to be met by the exporter. For example, there are strict fire regulations imposed on all children's toys in Germany. As all countries have regulations to some degree, check before you export your goods that there are no regulations or if so, what they are by contacting the Technical Help to Exporters section of the British Standards Institution. They will provide you with details of what countries control individual products and the points you must check. You will have to pay for detailed answers to how your produce may be affected in any one country, but the service is invaluable.

Customers abroad may demand changes in many goods to suit their tastes. If you produce clothing you may have to vary the weights of cloths to suit local climatic conditions. You may also have to alter sizes and cuts because the average size and shape may vary from country to country. Moreover, in many countries quantity is important in that not everyone can afford to buy much at a time. Cigarettes, for example, are often sold singly, as are razor blades, which need individual packaging. Packaging, especially of foodstuffs, may also have to conform with local regulations. The goods may have to be renamed or trade marks altered should they be unsuitable when rewritten in the local language.

Your aim, however, must be to sell where you have to make the fewest number of changes to what you produce, because such changes increase your production costs, often out of all proportion to the size of the changes made. Hence the suggestion that you find customers as close in all ways to your domestic customers as possible.

Export merchants

There are two other possibilities for exporters, the first being for those whose skills are in selling rather than in manufacturing. In this case you can set up as an export merchant, buying in from suppliers in the UK, or indeed from any part of the world, and reselling to customers overseas. Merchants do carry out a great deal of export work, and if you wish to develop a merchanting export business get in touch with the British Exporters Association.

Exporting unlabelled goods

The second possibility is for those whose skills are mainly in manufacturing and who might wish to concentrate on this aspect of exporting. In this case exporters can offer to make goods for sale by customers under their own labels or names. You may supply in bulk and leave the local buyer to package as he wishes. Or you may supply goods which only need labelling, such as clothes.

In both these cases you are concentrating on either selling or manufacturing and many companies would agree that it is better to do what you can do best, rather than try to do it all. Many Japanese successes have been built on one company making goods and another selling them.

WHO TO EXPORT TO

Having decided what and where to export you must then pin-point the customer to whom you wish to sell.

This person will not necessarily be the same as the user because with consumer goods and durables the goods may pass through several hands before they reach the actual user. Sweets, for example, will go from an importer to a wholesaler, and on to a retailer before reaching the hands of the child who eats them. But with many capital goods and raw materials the customer may well be the user, because he buys, for example, some machinery to manufacture things he proposes to sell.

As a small business you will be concerned primarily with your actual customers, and here you have a choice depending on what you sell and where you sell.

Selling to manufacturers or export agents

In the first place you need not go outside your own domestic ter-ritory to export, because you can sell components to other manu-facturers who incorporate them into the finished article, which is then exported. Having started this way you can expand to selling those components to manufacturers overseas. Second, you may supply export merchants with goods and leave them to sell them to their customers overseas. Merchants buy and resell for their own account. There are also 'confirming' houses who buy on behalf of principals overseas. In both cases you are relieved of all shipping and documentation problems, and are paid promptly in the UK. If this kind of exporting appeals to you contact the British Exporters Association. They will put you in touch with their members who specialise in your type of goods. Moreover, they can provide services like finding you an export manager to work for you on a purely part-time basis (often only being paid a commission). Department stores overseas also have representatives and merchants buying for them, so here you can start exporting by dealing with people and companies in the UK – an ideal way to start for a small company with limited money and manpower.

Commission agents and distributors

When a small company starts to develop business more extensively in one or two parts of the world, it can consider appointing an agent of some kind to represent it there, and get more business. For capital goods usually a commission agent is appointed, i.e. one who obtains orders for his principals, has them executed by the exporter direct to the customer, but who is paid a commission for every order he obtains. Commissions vary from 2.5 per cent to 15 per cent depending on the goods, the territory and problems of selling. For consumer goods a distributor is more common, i.e. one who buys goods from the exporter and resells them for his own account, making his money on the difference between the cost of the goods and their resale price locally. Both commission agents and distributors are widely used by small companies in export, the main problem being that there are so few good ones available. The DTI will help you to find them through its Export Representative Service, for which there is a charge if they find someone suitable. You must give these overseas agents every assistance; you must visit them regularly to keep them up to scratch; and you should really only consider them in your best overseas markets.

Using your own salespeople

As an alternative, and this might well apply within other EU countries, why not use your own salespeople? True, you may have a language problem, but there are always interpreters if your customer does not speak English or your people cannot manage the local language. But increasingly people are learning each other's languages in the EU. And as no one sells better than a company trained and employed person, every effort should be made to use the same sales force in the EU as at home. That is a proper integration of effort.

There are two instances where direct selling is most important. One is where services are concerned, because most exported services are one-offs, i.e. tailored to the exact requirements of the buyer. The other is where technical goods are concerned, and as many small companies deal with these, it is important that whoever deals with the customer overseas is technically competent. This is a weakness with many commission agents and distributors, and it really takes an engineer, for instance, to sell to an engineer. So if you wish to export highly technical goods or services you should consider using your own personnel to do the selling.

Information on opportunities

Of course, there are many opportunities occurring all the time overseas for business and you can, instead of concentrating on any particular part of the world, deal with opportunities as they arise. To be aware of them you have two good sources of information. The first is the OTS's Export Intelligence Service, which brings you (via computers) details of all published requests for goods all over the world.

Joint ventures

Another option of finding and dealing with customers overseas is to set up a small joint venture with a local small company. This is not as daunting as it may appear, and it may well be the answer for small businesses in specialised fields in the EU. One of the advantages here is that the UK exporter will then have the chance of expanding his domestic business by selling his partners' goods in Britain, while they sell his in their countries.

Your options

Do not think that you have to choose from these options. Most companies use some or all of them depending on where the customers are. For example, start by getting all you can out of export merchants and confirming houses. Start selling to the representatives of overseas department stores in Britain before tackling the stores in their own countries for greater business. Only select and appoint commission agents or distributors where you can find good ones and where you have gained some business. Use your own sales staff where you can see a need for them, preferably not too far away, and especially in highly technical fields. Perhaps develop joint ventures where you can find willing partners with similar interests to your own.

THE INTERNET

One of the most important developments in business over the last few years has, of course, been the proliferation of the Internet (covered in more detail in Chapter 12). More and more small firms now have a Web site which provides information about themselves and their products.

In a sense, having a Web site is akin to having a permanent stand at a trade fair or exhibition. You can explain and demonstrate your products and make direct sales (via interactive dialogue with customers). Internationally a site on the World Wide Web can give your business a vast potential reach, while the same messages can penetrate the narrowest of niche markets among information seekers.

There can be no doubt that the Internet greatly eases the marketing tasks of firms wishing to export. It removes all geographical constraints and permits the establishment of virtual branches instantly throughout the World and allows direct and immediate foreign market entry to the smallest of businesses. An Internet connection substantially improves communications with foreign customers, suppliers, agents and distributors, helps identify new customers and distributors, and can be used to generate a wealth of information on market trends. Arguably the availability of the Internet removes 'at a stroke' a number of the organizational and resource constraints supposedly associated with exporting.

PRICES AND TERMS

As you most certainly know, if you can estimate your costs of producing goods accurately, can fix a price to suit your customers and allow for a reasonable margin for yourself, then your sales are extremely worthwhile. This is easier said than done, but must be your aim in starting to export.

Allocating costs and deciding prices

You must first allocate some proportion of your fixed costs, or overheads, to export. As your exports grow you must increase this amount so that exports bear their full share of these costs. Next, you must calculate the variable costs of producing the goods for export, allowing for any extra costs due to changes to the goods being made to suit conditions locally. Hence you will take into account the raw material costs and labour costs plus any additional selling costs. Then allow for some reasonable margin as a contribution to the company's revenue, and altogether you should have a price at which to export. You must decide whether you will go for a small margin on a large volume of goods or a large margin on a small volume, but you will have most likely already decided that for your domestic trade. And if you are going to concentrate on EU business you must try to have your export prices much the same as those for the UK because in a Single Market customers will expect to pay the same prices for goods wherever they may buy them in Europe. This will become a vital consideration as the single European currency comes into circulation.

For most parts of the world you should calculate minimum and maximum prices, because many overseas buyers like to bargain, as in some countries that is how they customarily do business. You must take into account what buyers are prepared to pay, and this may well vary from country to country outside Europe. And you must take account of three additional factors when agreeing a final price. The first is when the order is to be placed, because in these days of ever-increasing prices most quotations should be limited to three or six months. The sooner a customer orders the lower the price. Second, how a customer is going to pay is important because export customers do take longer to pay, and if you can arrange payment when you ship the goods this is better than after the goods arrive. Third, you may well have to offer credit, and this is fine provided that the cost of such credit is reflected in the price.

Giving overseas customers quotes

Having arrived at a series of prices you must then decide how to quote your customers overseas. You will need to use one of the internationally accepted terms of delivery, known as Incoterms (these have been codified under that name by the International Chamber of Commerce). You should obtain a copy of the latest edition of Incoterms from the International Chamber of Commerce (ICC) in London. Normally you quote as your customer requests but, if he leaves it to you, most exporters quote FOB (free on board) except for Europe where it is becoming usual to quote DDP (delivered duty paid) because no duties are payable on goods in Europe, although you must remember that VAT or its equivalent is added everywhere.

For Europe your customers will prefer a quotation in their own currency or in Euros and this you may safely give provided you use what is called the forward rate of exchange. That will be explained later, under payment and finance. Customers in other parts of the world may also wish for a quotation in their own currency but you can only do this safely if there is a forward rate of exchange, and this applies only to the major currencies used in international trade. You can always use US dollars if no forward rate exists. You normally use a pro forma invoice when quoting, and you add to the cost estimated freight and insurance charges if you are quoting FOB although these are included if you quote DDP.

You should also include your conditions of sale as at home, and your lawyer should be able to suggest these, in order to protect you from unscrupulous customers overseas.

_____

Pricing services

If you sell services you will also have to arrive at a price based on your costs and a reasonable margin of return for yourself. But the basic rules remain, especially allowing for maximum and minimum prices to leave room for manoeuvring, since all services depend very much on who is selling them, and how far the buyers appreciate the variations in prices that so often occur. Hence you must try to get the best possible price, and no one can do this better than the person who actually provides those services.

Pricing licences

When you sell a licensing agreement you must put a price on the licence which will be a down payment in cash for the actual licence. This may be difficult to establish but will depend on the value of the process, trade mark, trade name, etc. Having arranged this you must negotiate an annual royalty on sales, at so much a unit. You must also insist on a minimum annual sales royalty, because licensees have been known to buy the licence merely to keep the goods off the market because they have a competitor. In addition you must agree the terms on which you will supply any raw materials, assuming the licensee is prepared to buy these from you. Your costs will be minimal, since you are merely supplying what you already possess, so that whatever you get from selling the licence to manufacture and sell overseas is more or less profit to you. But, of course, any license agreement will be for a long time so that you will not be able to take back the licence at a later date.

Pricing and selling in export is no different from domestic business. You will find, however, that a greater degree of flexibility in pricing may be required with overseas buyers who are more used to trading (that is, bargaining) than buyers in the UK. But this is for many companies part of the pleasure of exporting.

PHYSICAL DISTRIBUTION

If you make and export goods overseas, or act as a merchant by buying in your goods to be exported, you will need to arrange to have them transported to your customers in other parts of the world. You will also be concerned with the documents required in international trade, and you will need to ensure that the goods are insured against loss or damage while in transit. While you may sub-contract some of this work, you must know how to brief the people doing it for you, and there are certain things you will have to do yourself because the service cannot be provided.

Use of freight forwarders

In arranging transport, a company new to export should not engage special staff to do this, but should use the services of an expert. Such people are known as freight forwarders. You should, therefore, contact the British International Freight Association and ask them to recommend several of their members to you, after you have given some idea of the extent of the services you will be requiring, and the likely volume of your shipments. You then visit each and after discussing your problems with them and evaluating the services they can offer, and the charges they will make, you choose one to act for you. You must make this choice carefully because it makes no sense to obtain business from customers overseas, only to lose it because the physical transportation and documentation required are unsatisfactory.

What a freight forwarder can do for an exporter:

☐ suggest the best means of transport;
☐ book transport for you and pay advances on your behalf;
☐ documentation and ensuring that goods are put on the ship or aircraft;
☐ advise on suitable means of packing for insurance purposes;
☐ provide the necessary transport documentation after shipment;
☐ insure goods on your behalf;
☐ deal with customer clearance.

You, on the other hand, must brief your forwarder fully about the services you need for each shipment you wish him to handle, and this means having someone on your staff who can do this. Moreover, you must remember that there are certain things a forwarder cannot do: one is obtain payment for you; another is prepare the original commercial invoices, although he can handle specialised invoices such as those requiring signature by a Chamber of Commerce.

For these services he will charge and this will usually be a percentage of the freight costs involved, plus any extra costs where specialised documents have to be obtained. Is this cost-effective? For small companies the answer is almost certainly yes, especially as you will have more than enough to do to obtain payment and new orders, which you do not wish to lose because you failed to deliver promptly and efficiently.

If you are thinking in terms mainly of selling in the EU, the value of a good freight forwarder may well increase because many of them have organised their own road and rail services into Europe, as well as having special arrangements for shipments by air. To give quick and efficient service to customers in Europe you must examine all these new services offered by forwarders and make the best possible use of them. Many have extended these services to other parts of the world, and with the proliferation of transport services owing to an increased amount of international trade, the use of experts such as freight forwarders seems essential for most exporters.

Many small companies have been discouraged from starting off in export by the thought of additional paperwork, numerous complicated documents and horrific tales of shipments going wrong and customers demanding damages, etc. It need not be like this if you spend a little time learning what is involved in using a forwarder, whom you trust and pay well, to do it all for you.

If as a result of starting in export you also become involved in importing, for instance buying raw materials from overseas, you will almost certainly need someone to clear goods through Customs when they reach this country. Here the services of a freight forwarder are essential for any company.

PAYMENT AND FINANCE

For a small company tackling export for the first time being paid is a vital part of the business, because small companies cannot afford to incur bad debts or wait long for payment from customers. Most banks have a mass of helpful literature on methods of payment for exports, and you should ask your own bank for their booklet. You will in any case need to use your bank to obtain payment for your exports so talk to them at some length. Moreover, you may need their help to finance your new export trade.

Use of factors to handle payment

As with physical distribution you can, of course, opt out of handling payment from overseas by using a factor to do this work for you. A factor quite simply takes over all accounts receivable as the invoices are issued and is then responsible for collecting the money from the respective customers. But he will pay the exporter as soon as the invoices are ready, so there is neither any risk of non-payment nor any delay in the exporter getting his money. Factors deal with all problems of foreign currencies or lack of funds being transferred from overseas so you have no worries on this score. You may borrow from the factor and all you have to do is to pay the factor for the service, which can, however, be quite costly. You should bear in mind that customers may not like having a factor or his local representative chase them for the money. Moreover, you may not be allowed to deal with a particular customer if the factor feels he may be a bad risk. There are an increasing number of factors and you should obtain competitive quotations before deciding on one, if this is the way you wish to handle your payments for export.

Handling payment yourself

If you wish, on the other hand, to look after the payment yourself, and many companies new to export do, then you have several ways in which to do this. First, you can demand payment in advance. If you sell by mail order you may do this, using internationally accepted credit cards as the means of payment. But normally customers will not pay in advance. Do not accept a deposit and a promise of the remainder unless this is secured with a bank guarantee.

Second, do not offer open account terms to any customer unless you know him and are certain that he will pay. Ultimately, of course, you will have to treat customers in the EU this way as you do customers in the UK, but initially treat all customers, including those in Europe, with some caution. After all, they may well be late in paying and six months' delay in payment means, as you may know, that most of your profit has gone.

There are two generally accepted means of getting paid from overseas. The first of these is a documentary letter of credit, explained in the booklet _Uniform Customs and Practice for Documentary Credits_, published by the International Chamber of Commerce (ICC). Briefly, your customer opens a credit in your favour, which should be irrevocable and confirmed by a bank in the UK. This means that, provided you carry out the instructions contained in that credit, i.e. sending the goods as ordered, and provided the bank confirms the credit with the documents requested, you are sure to be paid. And this is usually soon after the goods have been shipped. But you must remember that all the shipping documents will have to go to the bank which has confirmed or advised you of the credit in the UK. And all the other instructions must be carried out, such as shipping by a certain date, etc. So make sure that everyone concerned with the shipment knows all the requirements of the credit.

Instead of a letter of credit you may obtain payment by means of a draft or bill of exchange. This is a document the exporter makes out, in effect asking the buyer to pay a certain sum of money for goods or services supplied, either at sight or at so many days after sight. The normal system is that the exporter collects together all the documents to enable the buyer to take delivery of the goods, and sends them to his own bank which passes them to a bank in the buyer's country. That bank in turn offers them to the buyer, handing over the documents if the buyer either pays or agrees to pay the amount of the draft. Hence the exporter can give a customer credit yet be more or less sure he will be paid. All this is fully explained in the ICC's booklet _Uniform Rules for Collections_. For a brief, but useful, summary of these matters, have a look at the book _Getting Started in Export_ published by Kogan Page.

Credit insurance

These are the most common ways by which buyers pay exporters and, while with a confirmed irrevocable letter of credit there is no risk of non-payment, if the credit is unconfirmed and if payment is being made by means of a bill of exchange, there is the risk that the money may not be transferred to the exporter's country because of some action by the government to prevent this (as, for example, with the Argentine at the time of the Falklands war). In both these cases the exporter should take out some form of credit insurance. The main body doing this is NCM Credit Insurance Ltd, a company that took over the short-term insurance business of the government-owned Export Credits Guarantee Department in 1991. NCM will pay 85 per cent of the value of the goods if the buyer cannot or will not pay or the money cannot be transferred to the seller. It also offers its customers domestic as well as foreign credit insurance. ECGD itself today concentrates on the insurance of payments for long-term capital projects, especially to non-Organisation for Economic Cooperation and Development (OECD) markets.

Apart from NCM, several other bodies offer export credit insurance, notably Trade Indemnity plc. Your normal broker should be able to provide you with information or alternative export credit insurers. You will need credit insurance when selling outside Europe, especially where there is a currency risk, but it is less essential when trading in the EU. The question of quoting in a customer's currency (or in Euros) has already been mentioned, and the system is that you ask your bank for a forward exchange rate which you use in your quotation. At the same time as you get the order you make a contract with your bank to sell that amount of foreign currency around the date you expect to receive it. The bank will then exchange the currency at the forward rate, irrespective of what the rate is on that day. But you must sell when you agree to or you are breaking the contract.

When you obtain an accepted bill of exchange, stating that your customer has agreed to pay you at so many days after seeing it, remember this is a valuable document because you can take it to the money market and exchange it for cash – not the full amount but at a discount. This means that you can give credit and get your money quickly, and you should allow for this in your prices.

PROMOTING YOUR EXPORTS

You clearly cannot expect your goods or services to sell themselves overseas however well known they may be at home. So you will have to go out and persuade people to buy them. First, you should try to do a good deal of selling yourself. This may not be as difficult as it sounds because, while language may be a barrier in some cases, interpreters are usually available and technical people nearly always understand each other. Learn to say a few words in any language where you have customers, but then revert to English for the negotiations. Do not be overawed by the immense amount you feel you should know.

You are unlikely to be able to allocate much money to spend on other forms of promotion, but you should try to make available as much money for export promotion as you allow, relatively speaking, for domestic business. Hence if you advertise, for instance, in some technical publications in Britain, you should also do so in countries where you hope to export. You can do this through your domestic advertising agency, who should know how to cope.

You may wish to book some space at a trade fair or exhibition overseas, both to meet customers and to publicise your goods. Check with the OTS first because they have a number of schemes whereby you can take part in these exhibitions at a reduced cost, and where a British exhibition is being organised you can become part of that for a minimal cost. If you wish to make contacts to sell in Eastern Europe taking a stand at the Leipzig Trade Fair is an excellent way of doing it.

You should take every advantage of free publicity for your company and the goods or services it exports by contacting the Central Office of Information. They are experts in obtaining free publicity in magazines and newspapers, on radio and television all over the world. All they ask is that you send them details and photographs, etc. of what you offer and they will send this information out to the world media free of charge.

You will certainly require some literature in other languages and you must make sure that the words and pictures you use are suitable for any particular part of the world. While there are many translation bureaux in Britain it is generally better to have someone rewrite what you wish to say locally, and then check that what has been said is exactly what you intend. It is probably also better to have the literature printed locally, both to avoid printing errors and to save customs duties, which are often high on imported sales literature.

BUDGETS AND PLANS

No one in a small company has much time to prepare elaborate plans and budgets, but if you propose to start off in export seriously you will need to work out a simple budget, together with a strategy to show how you propose to achieve your targets. This also helps to keep you on target and equally to show you if anything is going badly wrong.

Start by preparing a simple quantified objective for the year ahead. This need show no more than what you hope to export, and what you propose to contribute to the company's revenues.

Then work out a budget which should consist of, first, the revenue you estimate you will receive from export. This gross revenue should be all the money which will be coming in. From it deduct the cost involved in producing this revenue, i.e. the production costs, both fixed and variable, and any additional selling costs. Then deduct any money needed for promotion, and you will arrive at a net contribution to revenue. This should be more than the costs or starting off in export will not have been worthwhile.

Having set out your objective and your budget, jot down the strategy by which you propose to achieve these results. This list should include:

- [ ] where you propose to try to export;
- [ ] what you propose to export;
- [ ] to whom you are going to sell;
- [ ] at what prices and terms;
- [ ] how you will arrange transport if goods are involved;
- [ ] how you will get paid;
- [ ] how you will promote your sales.

_____

Try to set down some form of monitoring for the results so that you can see at a glance how you are progressing, and then, if necessary, you can halt what is in progress to see where the fault lies should things begin to go badly wrong.

As time goes by and you begin to integrate your exports in Europe more closely with domestic sales, you will have achieved a significant step forward, and you can begin to integrate all export sales with those in Britain, because a customer is a customer, irrespective of nationality or country of origin.

MANAGEMENT AND STAFF

Do not immediately engage more staff if you start to export. Explain what you are doing to your existing staff and find out if any member of staff has any particular interest or abilities in export. For instance, how many can speak another language? Would any of them be interested in handling any special aspect of export? In this way export will become part of your business rather than an extraneous area which you have tacked on to it.

Where you need help, buy it in from outside – for example, using the services of a freight forwarder to handle the physical distribution side. Buy in research but make the fullest possible use of all the help that is available to small businesses, both to tackle Europe and to expand elsewhere in the world.

When you have visitors from overseas, introduce them to your staff, since buyers like meeting people with whom they deal in correspondence but rarely meet. Moreover, it keeps the staff interested in the export side of the business and encourages them to put care and effort into serving your overseas customers.

Take advantage of the many courses in export practice and procedures run by Chambers of Commerce. If you wish to learn a little more about exporting, obtain the book _Getting Started in Export_, published by Kogan Page, which is written specifically to help small companies start off in export.

Appendix III lists under Export all the organisations mentioned in this chapter and gives their addresses and telephone numbers.

Checklist: Preparing for export

☐ Talk to your accountant about the costs of the project and the facilities you may need.

☐ Contact your Chamber of Commerce to see if it has an Export Development Adviser.

☐ Research your market. Check on local conditions, find out if your goods are suitable, and how they will be sold and what prices will be acceptable to customers.

☐ Examine the exports of British goods in your field to identify potential markets.

☐ Identify relevant local regulations or customer preferences and modify your goods accordingly.

☐ Investigate the potential of setting up a Web page on the Internet

☐ Identify a freight forwarder through the British International Freight Association.

☐ Consider which method of payment you will want to use and whether or not you will want to employ a factor to handle your payments for export.

☐ Research overseas trade fairs and exhibitions and contact the Central Office of Information to take advantage of free publicity.

☐ Draw up a budget and strategy for the year ahead and identify objectives.

☐ Discuss your plans with your staff and identify how many can speak another language and if any would be interested in handling special aspects of export.

12 Managing Communications and Information Technologies

As we advance towards the paperless economy, office systems are relying more heavily on information and communication technologies (ICTs). Playing an increasingly vital role in standard working practices, ICTs are contributing directly to business success and are likely to be a major factor determining competitive advantage as we move into the 21st century.

In particular, small to medium-sized enterprises stand to benefit from new technologies, such as computer networking and the Internet, which can improve efficiency, increase productivity and create an opportunity to gain real competitive advantage. The key is the potential of ICT's offer to share information.

Business use of technology is growing rapidly among small and medium-sized enterprises (SMEs). 'Moving into the Information Age', a 1998 DTI annual International Benchmarking Study, revealed that 86 per cent of all businesses think that information and communication technology is important to business success. The same survey revealed that over a third of SMEs now have Internet access. There is a whole range of ways in which IT is helping businesses to increase the speed and efficiency of their working practices. E-mail and fax, the Internet, video conferencing and networking are just some of those that are becoming commonly used. These applications lead to savings in time – and therefore costs – and make doing business quicker, easier and more competitive. Failure to exploit these opportunities could lead to the erosion of UK competitiveness. If other countries take greater advantage of the benefits of new ICTs UK companies will get left behind.

WHAT SCHEMES ARE AVAILABLE FOR SMES?

A helping hand for UK businesses exists in the Government-led Information Society Initiative (ISI) – a public-private partnership run by the Department of Trade and Industry. The aim of ISI is to promote the progress of UK businesses, particularly SMEs, towards the Information Age. Nationally, ISI seeks to raise awareness in a number of ways: a business Infoline (0345 15 2000), which gives information on programme activities has dealt with over 30,000 enquiries to date and an ISI Web site (http://www.isi.gov.uk) has been visited by some 70,000 users. A wide range of materials giving basic, jargon-free information to companies is also available.

The Information Society Initiative is supporting Business Links (and equivalents elsewhere in the UK) to set up dedicated ISI Local Support Centres (LSCs). At these centres local firms can obtain experience of, and advice on, networked technologies.

The nation-wide network of 80 centres offers impartial advice to companies on how technology can best be incorporated within a business strategy. Advising on everything from Internet access and Web page design through to help with Millennium compliance, they provide jargon-free consultancy and practical solutions tailored to the specific needs and aspirations of individual businesses. The ISI centres are aimed at all businesses ranging from those which do not use any IT, through to specialist multimedia hardware and software developers.

WHAT BASE-LINE EQUIPMENT IS NEEDED?

Getting started on the Internet is easier than you think. The requirements to get up-and-running are basic. As a small or medium-sized company you need only invest in the following:

- ☐ *A computer.* Either a PC with at least a 386 processor or a Mac with at least 8Mb of internal memory (RAM). To enjoy the more visual aspects of the World Wide Web you will need a machine with sufficient memory to be able to make full use of a graphical interface like Windows.
- ☐ *A modem.* The device which links the computer to the telephone network and can be either internal to the PC or external (connected by a cable). Speeds vary and while low speeds can be sufficient for simple e-mail, if you intend to download large files or use the Web you should usually go for the fastest modem you can afford.
- ☐ *A standard phone line.* Where the speed of access is important an ISDN line (Integrated Services Digital Network) should be considered.
- ☐ *An account with an Internet Service Provider (ISP) or on-line information provider.* There are over 100 ISPs in the UK. Typical subscription rates are between £10 and £12 per month. However, it is essential to compare what you are getting for your money to ensure you are achieving best value.
- ☐ *Appropriate software.* This would include a minimum connection software to manage the modem and to organise the dialling, an e-mail program and a Web browser. These are usually provided free by your ISP, included within subscription rates.

MARKETING AND EXPORTS

The Internet is a global network of computers with millions of users. It consists of many thousands of permanently linked powerful computers, called hosts. Anyone with a computer and modem can join this network by using a standard phone line. The

Setting up a business, no matter how small or large, is one of the biggest challenges that anyone can face. It can be rewarding, stressful, frustrating, fun or misery depending on the way the business is run and how successful it is.

Unfortunately, obstacles are often put in the way which need to be overcome before the business can move on and succeed. These can be large or small but, whichever, need to be overcome all the same. Increasingly, new businesses rely on the use of technology, in particular IT and communications, to maximise efficiency. This, however, can be a minefield - and an expensive one at that if you get it wrong. The use of PCs and mobile communications are almost fundamental basics for any business but many small businesses require more from technology than just the basics - they require a mixture of reliability, performance and mobility to offer the flexibility needed to keep several balls in the air at once.

Sony understand only too well the importance of reliability, performance and mobility. After all, it has built it's world renowned reputation on exactly those criteria - you only need to look at the worlds most successful consumer electronic product, the Sony Walkman, to understand this. However, Sony is known for more than just consumer products; Its Information Technology Division has been a world leader for over twenty years in the manufacture and supply of monitors and it's Trinitron, technology has revolutionised picture quality throughout the industry.

But Sony's Information Technology Division offers more than just monitors to help businesses run smoothly and efficiently. In 1998 Sony entered the Notebook PC market in style with the launch of its VAIO Notebook series. Not only does the VAIO range offer the style you would expect from Sony, it offers a whole host of features which makes it a truly outstanding choice for any business person on the move. Utilising the very latest in processing technology, disc storage, memory capability and audio visual performance, the VAIO range is a true workhorse, but it offers much more besides.

Creating a new market

The VAIO (Video Audio Integrated Operation) concept sees the convergence of existing IT and audio, digital and analogue technologies to deliver powerful business and home computing solutions. VAIO Notebook PCs offer full compatibility with other Sony products such as digital camcorders, cameras and mobile phones. Such devices plug straight into VAIO Notebooks and are instantly ready to communicate. Additionally, Sony has Introduced a 4-in-1 PC card modem which offers 56.6k modem transfer rates, 14.4k fax rates, is primed for Ethernet and ISDN connectivity and is GSM ready.

The VAIO range also includes notebooks which offer "Motion Eye' technology, a built-in video and stills camera. "Motion Eye" can capture digital still and motion pictures together with sound. Users can quickly and easily capture digital video clips and still pictures and send them via e-mail or include them in reports, sending virtually real time pictorial information whilst on the move.

The combination of these features means that, no matter where you are in the world, communication has never been simpler or more efficient. For small businesses this provides true portability and the ability to run the business whilst on the move. In fact, the ability to communicate visually or send and retrieve e-mails and faxes on the move by using a mobile telephone means that the traditional office environment could almost become redundant allowing for a truly mobile business.

Sony's comprehensive support through Club VAIO allows you to use your Sony equipment to its full potential. Completing the VAIO package is a host of software supplied with the range to enable connection to other devices via Sony's i.LINK interface, editing of video and pictures and communications management. Everything, in fact, that is required to fully utilise the features which make Sony's VAIO range unique in terms of interfacing and communications and with which Sony has created a new market in the technology sector.

Since it's launch the VAIO range has won award after award and has taken the retail market by storm. In January 1999 It was the best selling Notebook PC in retail (source: Romtec) - an unprecedented achievement in an industry which is fiercely competitive and which has been dominated for so tong by a very small number of manufacturers.

PCs and monitors have become such an everyday part of our working life that we can often overlook some important issues surrounding them and the use of them. When prices of such products are forced down we often look at pricing as the only factor and look for the 'best deal' possible. In some cases and for some applications this is understandable, but for the running of a successful business and for ensuring a healthy working environment then it is not always the most advisable approach. The reliability of any equipment purchased, especially when a company is in it's infancy is important; you don't want to be returning your equipment for a couple of weeks every time it breaks down.

With monitors, apart from the issue of reliability, there are environmental issues which can affect the health of users. Studies have been carried out by an organisation called TCO in Sweden which has resulted in the recommendation of numerous guidelines that monitor manufacturers should follow. These directly affect the overall picture quality of monitors and ensure that users do not suffer adverse reactions to sustained periods of use and, ultimately, that users time is more productive.

Sony's groundbreaking Trinitron technology was originally used in TV sets and set a new standard in picture quality.

It has been incorporated in to Sony's entire monitor range covering 15" to 21' as well as a SuperWide – 24". Sony's monitors compare very favourably in price with other monitor manufacturers but assure the user of quality and reliability. So when it's your business and there are better things to worry about then rest assured that Sony monitors will deliver the quality and reliability you need to focus on the issues that matter.

Sony - the big partner for small businesses

Sony is one of the biggest manufacturers of consumer electronics and IT equipment in the world - but Sony understands the issues of being small. When it comes to IT equipment, reliability, performance and mobility are key requirements to the successful and efficient running of any business - especially the small business.

Choose Sony as your partner for IT

The VAIO
range offers ultra-portability
without sacrificing performance. It's

'The best sub-notebook we've ever seen'

Best Ultra Portable System
VAIO Note PCG-505G
PC Magazine, 1998

Recommended
VAIO Note PCG-505G
**Personal Computer World,
December 1998**

Recommended
VAIO Note PCG-505G
**PC Direct,
December 1998**

Most Desirable
VAIO Note PCG-505G
**Computer Shopper
December 1998**

Gold Award
VAIO Note PCG-505G
**PC Format
December 1998**

Editors' Choice
VAIO Note PCG-505FX
**PC Magazine
March 1999**

according to Personal Computer World magazine. PC Magazine awarded it **'Best Ultra Portable System'** in their 1998 Technical Innovation Awards. **'It's one of the most complete notebook packages around - you quite literally get everything you need in one box, with no extra costs besides the software you want to use'** (T3 December 1998). **'Sony has created as near a perfect portable computer as existing technology permits'** (Computer Shopper December 1998). For further information on these award winning products and your nearest stockist, call Sony on **0990 424 424** now.

SONY®

speed of this global network means that, depending on traffic, it can be just as quick for a user in Glasgow to access a computer in Sydney as one in Manchester. It makes it easier and cheaper to do business with companies in the supply chain, as well as with customers and potential customers on the other side of the world.

One of the clearest examples of the Internet's business potential is the rapid development of on-line commerce. People now use the Internet to sell things, order products and services, find information and send messages. The smallest companies sit alongside vast corporations. Your presence on the Internet can be as effective and profitable for your business as a multi-national's presence can be for it.

Thousands of companies now use the Internet for sales and marketing. With your own Web site, you can not only tell the world about your products or services, but also accept orders or requests for information automatically and for 24 hours a day, seven days a week. You can even build up useful market information by tracking visitors to your site. In fact, building a Web site is now becoming an intrinsic part of marketing activity, like producing a price list or company brochure. There's a danger that companies who ignore its potential will increasingly lose market-share to those who have got involved.

Many British retailers are already running sites that let their customers buy directly over the Internet. But there are numerous other opportunities for electronic commerce, such as electronic publishing of newspapers and magazines, electronic mail-order, which lets customers browse on-line catalogues, and customer help-desks where customers can leave questions via e-mail.

The Internet is a public network that anyone can access, so the issue of security is important. While this was a concern in the past, most modern browsers now have sophisticated levels of security built in so that no unauthorised person can read, forge or intercept an on-line transaction. The number of UK banks now offering on-line banking confirms their satisfaction with Internet security.

You can also advertise on the Web by placing banner advertising on other people's Web pages, which can be targeted at those who could be interested in your particular product or service.

Just like your phone number, your e-mail address uniquely identifies you from the millions of other users on the Internet and lets them send e-mail to you. As with any marketing tool, it is wise to talk to someone who understands the medium and how best your company can use it. Your ISI Local Support Centre will be able to help you.

IMPROVING COMMUNICATIONS

Networks

There are valuable benefits to be derived from putting a network into an office. This can be nothing more that two or more computers joined together by a cable. Running network software on each machine lets them communicate with each other and linked computers mean that users can share peripherals such as a printer or fax. They can also have common access to files, such as spreadsheets and word-processed documents or a company database.

A network allows people to share information more readily and therefore allows companies to work faster, more efficiently, communicate better and gain greater security (by being able to back up day files centrally). With the addition of a camera and microphones at each geographical location and the means to send the sound and pictures between them, this can be expanded to accommodate video conferencing.

Electronic mail

Electronic mail (or e-mail) lets you write a message on one computer and send it to a person on another computer, possibly attaching a document or files at the same time.

The message can be sent internally between computers arranged into a network or it can be sent externally over the phone line to a computer anywhere in the world, often over a global network like the Internet. If you already have an internal network, it is comparatively easy to link it to the phone network so your business can, from your computers, send and receive e-mail from all over the world. This is already very common in companies based in several geographical locations.

The Daily Telegraph

The Daily Telegraph
Guide to Taking up a Franchise
Colin Barrow, Godfrey Golzen and Helen Kogan

'A thorough guide recommended for anyone considering franchising.'
BUSINESS FINANCE

'A roaring success!'
INTERNATIONAL SMALL BUSINESS JOURNAL

For potential franchisees everywhere, this bestselling guide will tell you everything you need to know on:

- Available franchise opportunities
- Financing a franchise
- Evaluating a franchise
- Evaluating yourself
- Legal and tax considerations
- Training opportunities
- Opportunities overseas.

£11.99 • Paperback • ISBN 07494 2919 4 • 256 pages • 1999

KOGAN PAGE
120 Pentonville Road, London N1 9JN

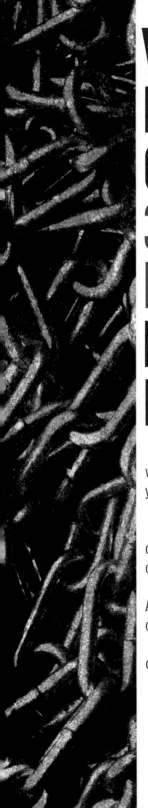

WHEN YOU'RE BREAKING OUT ON YOUR OWN, 30% OFF YOUR PHONE BILL MAKES A BIG DIFFERENCE

Suddenly all the economies that were irritating when you were on a payroll, begin to make sense when you have to pay yourself.

Like only making necessary phone calls.

But now there's no need to cut down on the number of phone calls you make. Or to compromise on service or reliability.

Just arrange to route your calls through the America 4 network and start saving up to 30% on your calls. Up to 50% on your mobile bills.

It won't cost you a penny to set up and once it's done, you can forget about it.

And start economising on paperclips.

Call free on 0800 583 1234.

America First. 1 Exchange Tower, Harbour Exchange Square, London E14 9GB. Tel:0171 577 7575 Fax: 0171 515 4849
email:sales@amer1ca.com

A distinct attraction of e-mail is that it is inexpensive and the cost is the same regardless of distance. It costs the same to send a message to Washington Tyne and Wear as is does to Washington DC because your connection is charged at local telephone rates. It is also fast. An e-mail can often reach its recipient in minutes, or at most within a few hours, even for those going to someone on the other side of the world.

E-mail is also convenient and flexible. Recipients don't have to be there to receive messages. They will be stored until needed and sending communications to large numbers of people is straightforward, with most software offering mailing-list features. You can also send computer files such as spreadsheets or project plans which can be worked on by the recipient. Many e-mail programmes also offer facilities that include security functions.

Intranet

An Intranet is a specialised kind of network. Based on Internet technology, an Intranet acts for many companies as an internal communication tool, like an electronic noticeboard. One of the most powerful incentives for taking the plunge and getting an Intranet up-and-running is that your competitors may already be utilising its potential.

Fax

Fax machines still have an importance in business today, despite the spread of e-mail. They can send documents quickly to recipients who don't have e-mail facilities and can send documents which can't be easily converted to a digital format, for example documents which have originated on paper.

Video and data conferencing

Video conferencing is a technology that enables meetings to be held without having to get everyone together in the same room. A video link with a simultaneous audiolink allows teams and individuals to see as well as hear one another, wherever they are

_____

in the world. The great majority of video conferencing systems now offer data conferencing at the same time.

Data conferencing gives the same people the ability to exchange, transfer and work collaboratively on a range of documents and other applications, either alongside video or just using an audiolink. It is now possible to work on files such as spreadsheets, examine remote objects, annotate 3D graphics or even share videoclips without regard to the distance between them. It is this data sharing element which makes conferencing such a potentially vital business tool.

FUTURE DEVELOPMENTS

No one really knows exactly how the Internet, e-mail, video conferencing and the array of information technology applications will develop. However, it is known that companies of all sizes and in all sectors, from finance to manufacturing, are moving on-line on a daily basis.

In the space of just a few years, the Internet has become the most exciting medium for commerce and business communications. Banks now offer banking services on-line. Retailers sell everything from books to groceries from cheap travel to ice cream. The Internet offers one of the biggest commercial opportunities available.

As more and more people go on-line the potential is vast. With the growing numbers on the Net, the capacity of the network is sometimes tested as service providers catch up with phenomenal increases in demand. But delivery and transmission systems will improve: optical fibres, for example, which carry up to 500 million times more information than current conventional copper wiring promise faster access.

Increasing profits and competitiveness are the critical factors for any business. Doing business electronically is frequently cheaper, quicker, more responsive and more collaborative, improving profits and performance. Given the current size, future growth prospects and attractive demographics of the new media, can any company afford not to investigate the possibilities?

Marketing your work

By Anne Wakefield, Marketing Manager, Redstone Telecom

How having the right telephone number can help you market your business

If the US is anything to go by, and in business it frequently is, then the freephone number is likely to become as essential a business tool as the telephone or the PC. In the UK customers are already voting with their dialling fingers: 61% of consumers are more likely to call a company with a freephone number than a comparable competitor that does not have one (Redstone Telecom Survey, June 1998). In today's increasingly competitive business environment, that's a statistic that no one can afford to ignore.

Freephone numbers fall into the category of marketing numbers, in other words those telephone numbers that enable the person or company receiving a call to bear all or part of the cost of that call, in place of the caller. With a freephone number the entire cost of the call is paid for by the called party, so that the call is free to the caller.

Why freephone?

Freephone numbers are used for the following reasons:

- Increasing new business - Research has shown that consumers are more likely to respond to an advertisement if it contains a freephone number.
- Retaining customers - A freephone number encourages existing customers to keep in contact.

- Providing a national image - Freephone numbers, like other marketing numbers, have the advantage of not being geographically specific. This means that even a very small company can give the impression of being a national organisation, enabling it to compete with businesses much larger than itself.

Other marketing numbers include local and national rate numbers. A local rate number is where the cost of the call is shared between the caller and the called party. The caller pays a local rate for the call regardless of his geographic location. The remainder of the cost of the call is borne by its recipient. National rate provides a single, location independent number for all calls to a company, with callers paying the national rate, wherever they are dialling from in the UK. In this instance no costs are borne by the called party. With some telecoms operators, such as Redstone Telecom, businesses can actually earn money on national rate calls they receive.

Making marketing numbers work in practice

Correctly used, marketing numbers make compelling

business sense. It is however, essential to consider them as part of your entire business strategy in order to maximise their effectiveness.

Which is the best type of marketing number for my business?

Consider what you want to achieve by providing a number for customers to contact you. Are you trying to increase awareness of your company, to improve the quality of your customer service, or to broaden the reach of your business? A freephone or local rate number will help you achieve all these objectives.

Businesses for whom national rate numbers are a viable option are likely to be those that provide a unique or niche service, or those whose customers are not motivated by cost savings.

What can I afford?

The mostly widely known and understood type of marketing number is freephone, it is also the most expensive number to implement.

Calculate the number of calls you need to receive, the number of sales leads, and the number of actual sales you need to receive in order to make a return on your investment.

If you feel that the cost of introducing a freephone number cannot be justified, consider a cheaper option such as local rate.

How will the number fit into my marketing strategy?

If you acquire a new marketing number, you must tell people about it. Consider launching it to your target audience via an advertising or direct mail campaign.

Think of your marketing number as a market research tool as well. Use the customer information you gather from it to hone your future marketing activities to meet your customers' needs.

What are the potential pitfalls?

The most important things to ensure when setting up a marketing number are that you have put in place adequate resources to deal with the influx of calls and that all incoming calls are met with a helpful and friendly response.

How can I tell if the marketing number is working?

Monitor the number of calls you receive on your marketing number, and the outcome of each call. How does this compare to calls received on your normal business number or to previous advertising campaigns? Does the revenue being generated justify the outgoing?

If the response rates are not what you had hoped, look again at the way in which you are using your number. Who knows about it? Who is calling, and - more importantly - who is not calling? How could you improve the way you reach those people to let them know about your number and encourage them to call?

Using other telephone numbers to give that personal touch

Above we have discussed how marketing numbers can help prospects and customers contact your business, but let's not forget that there will also be times when they need to contact you personally. You may have a phone in the office as well as a mobile for when you are out and about, but that's at least two calls a customer may have to make to get in touch with you, and then there's no guarantee that they will have both numbers to hand. The more barriers there are to tracking you down, the more likely it is that they will simply not bother. With the aim of providing a solution to this issue, personal number services were launched in the UK in the early 1990s.

What is a personal number?

A personal number is a telephone number that is not linked to any fixed or mobile phone, nor to any region or location, instead it is linked to you. You simply programme it to follow your movements. Your calls are then diverted to your chosen fixed or mobile phone number, allowing you to give out just one number for people to contact you. Customers do not need to know where you are or indeed where you are going to be, so you can get on and do your work, be it at home, at the office or at another location, in the know ledge that when someone calls you on your personal number they'll be able to reach you.

Personal choice

The UK has led the way in Europe and as a result the personal number market in this country is well advanced. There is a variety of personal number options available from different telecoms operators, some are capable of tracking you down by calling a sequence of pre-programmed telephone numbers until you are found, which tend to be the most expensive option, others, such as the market leader, Callsure from Redstone Telecom, require you to manage where calls are received and are significantly less expensive.

Above all the aim of all these different telephone number services, is to provide you with an efficient and effective means to market your business and to profit from it.

About Redstone Telecom

Redstone Telecom offers a range of inbound and outbound telephony products to the domestic, small business and corporate markets, including a range of freephone, local rate, national rate and personal number services.

For further information about these and other services available from Redstone Telecom, please CallFree

08000 35 35 45.

Redstone Telecom
Numbers that improve
your bottom line

As a budding entrepreneur you're obviously going places.
We'll make sure all your calls follow you there.

Glad we've caught you. Running your own business obviously entails a lot of running around.
So we're pleased to grab a quick chance to tell you about Callsure from Redstone Telecom.
It's a cost-effective service that lets you divert all your calls via a single, personal number to any
phone, fixed or mobile, wherever you might be working, however temporarily. And once you've
made yourself nicely indispensable, we'll boost your new business drive with a freephone number to
make you even more attractive to your prospects. Interested? Then spare us a few more minutes on

CallFree 0800·0 35 45 55

www.redstone.co.uk

Whatever you're up to, we've got your number.

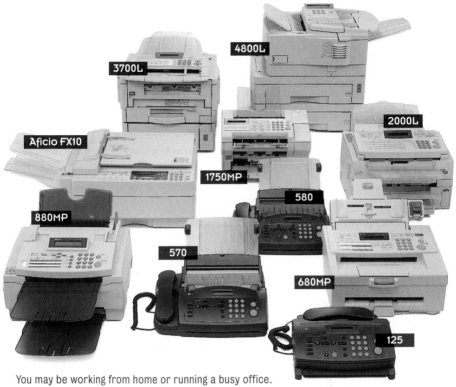

You may be working from home or running a busy office.

Whatever the circumstances, you can count on Ricoh for a fax machine that multiplies your productivity.

Just starting out? Ricoh has entry-level thermal and plain paper faxes that can double as a telephone, answering machine or occasional copier.

There are laser faxes for high volume and high quality. And for the ultimate in multi-functionality, Ricoh offers a digital number that networks with your PCs to print, scan and copy as well as fax.

When you add up all the possibilities, it's clear there's only one company worth talking to.

Call our number – 0800 30 30 50 – or send for full details on the Ricoh range. That way, you'll definitely be looking after No.1.

RICOH
Image Communication

Fax forward to the future.

A better lifestyle and real financial security, in your own independent business.

Whether you're looking to begin working for yourself, or wish to increase your earnings and financial security alongside your existing business, Euphony offers the perfect business opportunity.

Join Euphony as an Independent Euphony Consultant in your own part time or full time business, and make money simply by showing people you know how to save money off their BT phone bill.

When you connect people you know through Euphony, they keep their existing phone number and all the BT services they prefer. As their savings build, your own long term residual income builds too. It's the perfect business opportunity, making money simply by showing others how to save money!

A business for everyone.

It's a simple business too, one that anyone can enter, and when you do there are no products to stock, no deliveries to make, no invoicing, no territories or targets, no customer risk and no experience needed.

When you become an Independent Euphony Consultant, you'll be making money, and creating a more secure future for yourself. You'll also be joining a business that's growing faster than any other business in the UK telecoms sector!

Enter the telecoms business, no experience required!

To quote Ben Murtagh, an Independent Euphony Consultant from Northern Ireland: 'I'd been in sales all my life working with a food company, selling into supermarkets. It's a business that's seen wholesale changes, and at 52 I was concerned for my future.

...I first heard about the Euphony opportunity when I was visiting a local supermarket that was closing. The young manager explained he was going into the 'telecoms business', and made me realise I was capable of doing the same, even though I had no telecoms experience.

I now run my Euphony business full time, I love it, I get to meet lots of new people and I've also found the pension I've been looking for too!'

Support that spells success.

People from all walks of life have discovered that they can achieve their business ambitions through Euphony. It's a business opportunity that delivers a long term residual income, and enables everyone to work at their own pace. Doctors, marketing professionals, dentists, management consultants, trade professionals, even stay-at-home grandmothers have discovered that Euphony really is a different kind of company. Euphony offer quality training and connect you to a support network of like-minded people that makes building your own business very rewarding and very enjoyable!

A once in a lifetime opportunity.

Deregulation in the telecoms market has created a one-off opportunity that Euphony have capitalised on, developing one of the most exciting growth opportunities in the UK today. Euphony's success has shaken the telecoms industry, recording consistent, exponential growth since its launch in January 1998. Euphony is now on-track to become a major UK telecoms service provider, while also providing totally committed support to its Independent Consultants. It will also continue to strengthen the range of phone call savings it offers, as it continues to grow and develop, faster than any other business in the UK telecoms sector.

Take part in the perfect business opportunity today.

Connect to www.euphony.com today, you'll discover all the facts, and find out exactly how customers make consistent savings off their phone bills. You'll find out more about Euphony's perfect business opportunity, and you'll also find an Independent Euphony Consultant to talk to in your area. The Consultant you choose will answer any questions you may have, and will be able to show you just how simple it is, to join the most exciting business opportunity in the UK to date.

For a better lifestyle, and a long term residual income that creates a secure financial future, simply connect to your nearest Independent Euphony Consultant.

Simply call 0118 921 8500 today, or visit **www.euphony.com**

euphony
communications limited

...trust Euphony to get you better connected.

Can you afford not to be connected' with Euphony?

Safe companies have healthier profits

A survey for the British Safety Council has identified a group of small private companies as lethal weapons in their handling of health and safety at work.

"These are businesses that have very low regard for staff safety or the law, yet believe they know it all," said Sir Neville Purvis, Director General of the Safety Council. "They have no professional support. Although they might take some (free) advice from the Chamber of Commerce, they won't budget for safety training and have learned nothing from previous accidents."

The British Safety Council provides a range of services to educate all organisations, regardless of size, on the importance of best practice for successful businesses in increasing productivity and profitability and helping to win new contracts and repeat business.

A great

deal

While our competitors are shouting about low cost, RSL COM are talking about high value.

With operations in 21 countries across 4 continents and a valuation of over $1 Billion on the US NASDAQ stock exchange, RSL COM is the world's first truly global telecomms company now offering both fixed line and mobile services. And because we own our network, we can offer our customers highly competitive rates while maintaining high quality voice transmission.

 RSL COM Point of Presence (POP)

 RSL COM Planned POP

△ Internet Gateway

△ Planned Internet Gateway

Via RSL COM's growing points of presence we serve the national and international needs of almost 1 million customers world-wide. RSL COM's network is a massive infrastructure that blankets the globe, delivering calls in-country and to every other country in the world.

USEFUL CONTACTS AND ADDRESSES

If you are thinking of introducing new technologies into your workplace your first point of call should be your ISI Local Support Centre. Local Support Centres are being set up all around the UK in partnership with the Business Links in England and the equivalent organisations in Scotland, Wales and Northern Ireland. You can try out, first hand, technologies like e-mail and the Internet. The emphasis is on helping you make immediate and effective use of technology with guidance tailored to your individual business demands.

Ring the ISI Business Infoline on 0345 15 2000 to find out where your nearest ISI Local Support centre is. The ISI Web site is at: *www.isi.gov.uk*, e-mail: *info@isi.gov.uk*

England

For broad ranging advice, support and help with establishing your priorities, contact your local Business Link. Call the National Business Link line on 0345 567765 – they'll put you in touch with your nearest office. Visit the Web site at: *http://www. businesslink.co.uk*

Northern Ireland

The Industrial Research and Technology Unit (IRTU) can make you aware of the business benefits of using electronic communications and offer impartial advice.
Call the Superhighway Helpline on 0800 515319, e-mail: *superhighway.irtu@nics.gov.uk* or visit the Web site: *www.nics.gov. uk/irtu*

Scotland

Your Local Enterprise Company or Highlands & Island Enterprise can give you practical guidance, project support and impartial advice.

Lowlands: Sue Kearns at the Scottish office; tel: 0141 242 5527; e-mail: *Sue.Kearns@so049.scotoff.gov.uk*

Highlands and Islands: Stuart Robertson at Highland & Islands Enterprise; tel: 0345 573567; e-mail: *isiaware@hient.co.uk*

Wales

Business Connect will direct you to the particular service you need on specific information-based matters and in support of business activity more generally call Business Connect on 0345 969798. Visit the Web site at: *www.bc-wales.org.uk*

Other sources of information

BACT (Business Advisory Committee); tel: 0171 634 8773; Web site at: *www.acts.org.uk*

Checklist: Managing IT

- ☐ Contact ISI for information on IT or visit ISI Local Support Centre.
- ☐ Assess your needs before purchasing equipment, particularly with regard to how quickly you will need to receive and send material.
- ☐ Consider the type of computer and how big a memory you will require for your business needs.
- ☐ Spend time visiting other company web sites to assess if your company would benefit from having a presence on the Internet.
- ☐ Consider advertising your products by placing banner advertising on other people's Web pages.
- ☐ Consider ways in which to use communication tools such as networks and e-mail and whether it is cost-effective.

Appendices

APPENDIX I: THE COSTS OF DIFFERENT METHODS OF RAISING FINANCE

Type of finance	Description	Size of facility
Proprietor's own resources	Savings or personal borrowings	Dependent upon what investors can afford
Private investors	Savings or personal borrowings contributed by family, friends, business partners or acquaintances	No limit. If private investors seek tax relief under the Enterprise Investment Scheme (EIS) there is a limit of £150,000 per person per annum that is eligible
Bank overdraft and short-term loans	Short-term funding that should generally be used to cover short-term business needs. Can be withdrawn at any time	Depends upon the ability of the company to repay and the security available
Business loans from a bank	Unlike mortgages these have a defined term, usually between two and seven years	Usually from £5,000 upwards

Cost to the business	Timescale for applications	Terms and conditions
The income the money could have earned if invested elsewhere	Immediate	None
The interest or dividends that must be paid to investors Legal costs of producing a shareholders' agreement	May take a few weeks or months, depending upon the progress of negotiations	There is usually a shareholders' agreement and possibly amendments to the Articles of Association, which both govern the rights of the investors and the management. They may also restrict some management action such as limiting remuneration and borrowing powers
There is generally an arrangement fee, payable in advance, of around 1.25 per cent for new lending and 0.75 per cent for renewals. In addition there is a fee to cover the completion of any security Interest rates for new businesses vary between 2 and 6 per cent above bank base rates	Usually only a few days but may extend to several weeks depending upon any demands for property valuations or additional information, life insurance policies and legal process	The bank usually requires a debenture conferring a fixed and floating charge over the assets of the business. May also require directors guarantees. Will usually want regular accounts
There is generally an arrangement fee, payable in advance, of around 1.5 per cent Legal and possibly accountancy costs	Probably a couple of weeks to a couple of months. The bank will want to understand the expected cash flows from the business and will seek information to support this	A debenture giving a fixed and floating charge over the assets of the business to the bank

Type of finance	Description	Size of facility
Commercial mortgages	Available from banks, finance houses and insurance companies. Secured specifically on property assets Available for up to 20 years	Dependent upon the value of the property put up as security and upon the expected amount of cash flow from the business that will be available to pay interest and repay capital
Long-term loans	Usually provided by banks, insurance companies etc	Probably a minimum of £250,000
Bills of exchange	Usually used to finance a particular trade transaction, these are like cheques drawn on a bank but payable at a particular date and subject to certain conditions e.g. delivery of the goods. The recipient can get a bank to lend against one	Usually over £100,000. The amount depends upon the strength of the issuing and receiving company, since a default by either could invalidate the bill

Cost to the business	Timescale for applications	Terms and conditions
Commercial investigation, survey and legal costs are usually borne by the borrower and may amount to up to 2 per cent of the amount borrowed. In addition there may be an arrangement fee of up to 1.25 per cent Interest is charged at rates from 2 to 4 per cent above bank base rates: rates fixed for up to 5 years may be available	Several weeks, giving time for property valuation, internal approval procedures and a review of the expected cash flows from the business	Mortgage document will charge property to the lender. Other supporting security may sometimes be requested
Lower rates of interest than overdraft. May be available at fixed rates, in which case the rate depends upon market expectations of future movements in interest rates Valuation and legal costs together with some cost for the lender's commercial investigation	Two to three months. Can be longer for a large facility	A debenture will give the lender a fixed and floating charge over all the assets of the business
Discounts charged are equivalent to between 1.5 and 4 per cent over the three month inter bank rate There are no set-up costs	The initial facility may take a couple of weeks to establish	There will be an upper limit to the size of the bill that may be discounted. There may also be conditions relating to the type of transaction or customer financed in this way. The company effectively takes the risk on default on a bill of exchange

Type of finance	Description	Size of facility
Acceptance credits	Like a bill of exchange but with the addition of backing by a bank	Usually over £250,000
Factoring	A factoring house takes over the sales ledger for a company, an administration fee, and also advances up to 80 per cent of debtors when they are invoiced	There is usually a minimum annual turnover of £250,000
Invoice discounting	Similar to factoring but the finance house does not manage the sales ledger. It advances money against specific invoices, leaving it to the borrower to collect the monies	Up to 80 per cent of the value of agreed debts. Some discounters may also limit a facility to, say, 50 per cent of the total value of trade debtors
Hire purchase and lease purchase	Purchase of equipment, paid for by the finance house, which transfers ownership to the borrower with the final instalment	Usually less than £100,000 per item
Leasing	Generally available for two to seven years to finance plant and equipment. There may be an option to buy the equipment at the end of the term	Can range from hundreds of pounds to millions

Cost to the business	Timescale for applications	Terms and conditions
Acceptance commission is 0.5 to 2 per cent There may be a commitment fee, payable if the facility is not used	As for bills of exchange	There will be an upper limit to the size of bill that may be discounted. There may also be conditions relating to the type of transaction or customer financed in this way
Typically 2 to 4 per cent over finance house base rates (higher than bank base rate) plus a fee ranging from 0.75 to 3 per cent to manage the sales ledger There is usually a set-up fee of around 0.25 per cent of the opening debtors	Timescale depends upon the financial strength of the company, its trade, the number and nature of the company's customers and how much investigation is required. Can usually be done within a month	Can be arranged with no recourse against the borrower if the debtor does not pay but this costs more and a lower percentage of the debt is usually available for finance. Some debtors may not be accepted
Typically 2 to 4 per cent over finance house base rates (higher than bank base rate)	As for factoring	Can be arranged with no recourse against the borrower if the debtor does not pay but this costs more and a lower percentage of the debt is usually available for finance. Some debtors may not be accepted
Depending upon the covenant of the borrower, usually 2 to 5 per cent over finance house base rate	A few days or a week or two depending upon the size of facility and the standing of the borrower	The equipment belongs to the finance house and reverts to them if the borrower defaults; all payments up to that point are lost to the borrower. Equipment must usually be insured by the borrower
Between 3 and 6 per cent over finance house base rate. Fixed interest rates are sometimes available	For lower cost items such as cars, leasing may take only a few days to arrange but for large scale leasing it can take several weeks	Default may lead to repossession of the property by the leasing company. There may also be other business or even directors' guarantees to secure the leasing

237

Type of finance	Description	Size of facility
Contract hire	Regular hire payments that leave the ownership of the asset hired with the hire company	Can range from a few pounds to millions (eg for large computer installations)
Sale and leaseback	Sale of property or a significant item of machinery to a leasing company – it is immediately leased back	The size of facility can range from a few thousand pounds to millions. The market value of the asset defines the upper limit
Venture capital	Venture capital organisations will invest in shares and loans to a company. They will usually take only a minority stake and may form investment syndicates	There are limited numbers of institutions providing finance of less than £500,000 but there is no upper limit
Venture capital trusts	A special form of venture capital company that bears some restrictions to its operation in return for tax advantages to its investors	Limited to £1m invested in any one company

Cost to the business	Timescale for applications	Terms and conditions
From 2 to 5 per cent above bank base rates	From a few days to a few months for large transactions	There will usually be a minimum period for the hire contract and a lower rental available after that has expired
As for leasing There are also valuation costs and legal expenses on the sale and leasing agreement There may be a risk of a capital gains tax liability	This sort of transaction is usually more complex than ordinary leasing and will therefore take a couple of months or even more to complete	Standard leasing terms
Venture capital organisations will seek returns ranging from 20 to 40 per cent on *equity* investments. They will take this from dividends, interest and expected capital gains. Since entrepreneurs often seek returns of this scale they are not as high as they seem Legal and accountancy costs will be incurred and there will usually be a charge to cover the costs of the venture capital company	Investments rarely take less than six weeks to arrange	A formal agreement will cover matters such as: prevention of the proprietor from engaging in other business activities without permission, level of borrowing permitted, right for the vc house to be consulted on capital expenditure, levels of directors' remuneration and dividends, what happens if the business performance does not meet targets etc Some institutions want to be able to realise their investment in three to seven years and structure their terms to encourage this
As for venture capital	As for venture capital	As for venture capital

Type of finance	Description	Size of facility
Trade credit	This arises from using the time available before a supplier's invoice must be paid	Depends upon the size of the debts owed
Supplier discounts	Many suppliers will offer discounts for early settlement of their invoices	Depends upon the size of the purchase
Local authority grants	Some local authorities, particularly in poorer areas, will offer grants to assist local businesses e.g. building improvement or marketing assistance	Generally small scale – typically £5,000 to £10,000 maximum
Grants to assist business development and training	There are several schemes available through local Training and Enterprise Councils or Business Link as well as City Challenge for certain areas	Generally up to about £5,000
Landlords rent-free periods	Many landlords will allow new tenants in unlet developments to occupy property free of rent	The period may range from a few months to a couple of years
Consumer credit	It could be said that providing finance to the customers of a retail or mail order business is effectively financing the business	Generally up to £100

(Reproduced by kind permission of Robson Rhodes.)

Cost to the business	Timescale for applications	Terms and conditions
Delayed payment may lead to higher prices, reduced credit or a refusal to trade	n/a	As for venture capital
The cost of this financing is whatever interest could be earned on the money if the supplier was paid later	n/a	n/a
None	Generally a few weeks	The work must be carried out
None, although the funding may be available only on a matching of the company's investment	Generally a week or two but a consultant's report may be necessary	The company must carry out the training or formulate the business plan that is funded. The TEC may insist upon the use of its own or recommended consultants to carry out the work
The rent free period is often balanced by a higher rent in the future	This can take days or weeks: as long as it takes to negotiate a lease	No specific conditions although the benefit is often not transferrable if the tenant assigns the lease
None	Typically a few days	In some cases the finance house may seek the guarantee of the company for each customer

APPENDIX II:
FURTHER READING FROM KOGAN PAGE

Kogan Page publish a wide variety of helpful titles for people in business. A full list of titles is available by writing to the publisher at the address given on the back cover, by calling on 0171 278 0433 or by visiting Web site: www.kogan-page.co.uk

Leaflets from government offices provide a further source of information, either from the government department concerned or from the Stationery Office.

Business Communication

CBI Corporate Communications Handbook (1998), eds Timothy Foster and Adam Jolly
Doing Business on the Internet (1998), Simon Collin
How to be a Better Communicator (1996), Sandy McMillan
Marketing Communications 2nd edition (1998), Paul Smith
Sales Promotions 2nd edition (1998), Julian Cummins

Start-ups, Business Plans and New Directions

The Business Plan Workbook 3rd edition (1998), Colin Barrow, Paul Barrow and Robert Brown
Forming a Limited Company 6th edition (1998), Patricia Clayton
Great Ideas for Making Money (1994), Niki Chesworth
Money Mail Moves Abroad (1998), Margaret Stone
Net That Job! Using the World Wide Web to Develop Your Career and Find Work (1998), Irene Krechowiecka
Working for Yourself 19th edition (1999), Godfrey Golzen

Law and Company Secretarial

An A–Z of Employment Law: A Complete Reference Source for Managers 2nd edition (1997)
The Company Secretary's Handbook: A Guide to the Duties and Responsibilities 2nd edition (1998), Helen Ashton
Law for the Small Business 9th edition (1998), Patricia Clayton

Finance, Accounting and Bookkeeping

Accounting for Non-Accountants 4th edition (1999), Graham Mott
Do Your Own Bookkeeping (1988), Max Pullen
Financial Management for the Small Business 4th edition (1998),
Colin Barrow
Self Assessment for the Small Business and Self-Employed (1998), Niki
Chesworth
Understanding Company Accounts 4th edition (1995), Bob
Rothenburg and John Newman

Franchising

Guide to Buying Your First Franchise 3rd edition (1999), Greg
Clarke
Taking Up a Franchise 13th edition (1999), Colin Barrow and
Godfrey Golzen

Import and Export

CBI European Business Handbook 5th edition (1999), ed Adam Jolly
The EMU Fact Book (1998), Niki Chesworth and Susie Pine-Coffin
*The Export Handbook: In Association with the British Chambers of
Commerce* (1998), ed Harry Twells
Getting Started in Export (1998), Roger Bennett
Getting Started in Importing (1998), John Wilson

Management

*How to Be an Even Better Manager: A Complete A-Z of Proven
Techniques and Essential Skills . . . Reveals the Secrets of Successful
Managers* 4th edition (1994), Michael Armstrong
International Dictionary of Management 5th edition (1995), eds
Hano Johannsen and G Terry Page
Introduction to Modern Management (1998), Tony Dawson
Transform Your Management Style! (1998), Hilary Walmsley

Sales, Marketing and Advertising

Customer Driven Marketing: The Ideal Way to Increased Profits Through Marketing, Sales and Service Improvement (1997), John Frazier-Robinson

Do Your Own Market Research 3rd edition (1998), Paul Hague and Peter Jackson

European Direct Marketing Association 3rd edition (1999), eds Adam Baines and Sheila Lloyd

Handbook of International Direct Marketing: In Association with the 101 Ways to Boost Customer Satisfaction (1997), Timothy R V Foster

A Handbook of Marketing and PR for the Small Business (1998), Moi Ali

How to Sell More: A Guide for the Small Business 2nd edition (1997), Nei Johnson

101 Ways to Get Great Publicity (1992), Timothy R V Foster

A Marketing Action Plan for the Growing Business (1999), Shailendra Vyakarnam and John Leppard

Measuring Customer Satisfaction (1993), Richard F Gerson

Selling by Telephone, 2nd edition (1998), Chris de Winter

Successful Marketing for the Small Business: The Daily Telegraph Guide, 4th edition (1998), Dave Petten

Successful Marketing for Small Businesses 4th edition (1998), Dave Patten

Working From Home

Running a Home Based Business revised edition (1998), Diane Baker

Your Home Office: A Practical Guide to Using the Technology Successfully 3rd edition (1998), Peter Chatterton

APPENDIX III: USEFUL ADDRESSES

UNITED KINGDOM

Department of Trade and Industry

Provides advice, support and information, including Business Link, which helps small firms identify business problems, produce action plans and access a wide range of business support services. Enquiries: 1 Victoria Street, London SW1H 0ET (0171 215 5000). Small Firms and Business Link Division: Level 2, Department of Trade and Industry, St Mary's House, c/o Department for Education and Employment, Moorfoot, Sheffield S1 4PQ (0114 270 1356); Web site: www.dti.gov.uk. Provides a booklet, *A guide to help for small firms*, which gives an overview of Government action to help small firms, listing services and programmes available and contact points for further information, including addresses of Training and Enterprise Councils in England and Wales, Local Enterprise Companies in Scotland, and Business Links.

Training and Enterprise Councils (TECs) and Local Enterprise Companies (LECs)

Training and Enterprise Councils in England and Wales and Local Enterprise Companies in Scotland offer training and small business support to meet the needs of the local community. A list of these can be obtained from: Small Firms and Business Link Division, Level 2, Department of Trade and Industry, St Mary's House, c/o Moorfoot, Sheffield S1 4PQ (0114 270 1356). Web site: www.tec.co.uk

ENGLAND

Rural Development Commission

Government agency for co-ordinating the economic and social development of English rural areas. Also provides small factory units and workshops in Special Investment Areas and financial assistance to rural community councils and other bodies. Contact 141 Castle Street, Salisbury SP1 3TP (01722 336255) for advice on nearest local organiser. Web site: www.argonet.co.uk

English Tourist Board

Provides a wide range of expert advice on those involved in the tourism and leisure industry. Further information from Development Advisory Services Unit, Thames Tower, Blacks Road, Hammersmith, London W6 9EL (0181 846 9000).

WALES

Welsh Development Agency

Provides local companies with business development programmes, assists in developing international markets, helps in securing funding and financial support. Welsh Development Agency, Principality House, Friary, Cardiff, South Glamorgan CF1 4AE (0345 775577). Web site: www.wda.co.uk
Local Offices:
South Wales Division: QED Centre, Treforest Industrial Estate, Pontypridd, Mid Glamorgan CF37 5YR (0345 775577).
West Wales Division: Llys-y-ddraig, Penllergaer Business Park, Swansea SA4 1HL (01792 790000).
North Wales Division: Unit 7, St Asaph Business Park, St Asaph LL17 0LJ (0345 775577).

Development Board for Rural Wales

Help for small businesses in mid-Wales. Advisory service; factories and workshops; loans. For information: Marketing Director, Ladywell House, Newton, Powys SY16 1JB (01686 626965).

Wales Tourist Board

Advisory services unit to help new and existing enterprises in the tourist industry. Grants and loans available. Free advisory visits, leaflets and fact sheets. Seminars and farm tourism training courses. Brunel House, 2 Fitzalan Road, Cardiff CF2 1UY (01222 499909).

SCOTLAND

Scottish Enterprise

The Small Business Division offers professional advice and technical instruction to help develop small firms in rural and urban areas. Loans and other capital obtainable; small factories and workshops. 120 Bothwell Street, Glasgow G2 7JP (0141 248 2700). Web site: www.scotant.co.uk

Highlands and Islands Enterprise

Provides information on Local Enterprise Companies. Contact: Director of Industrial Development and Marketing, Bridge House, 20 Bridge Street, Inverness IV1 1QR (01463 234171). Web site: www.hie.co.uk

Scottish Tourist Board

Provides opportunities for marketing. 23 Ravelston Terrace, Edinburgh EH4 3EU (0131 332 2433).

NORTHERN IRELAND

Industrial Development Board for Northern Ireland

Help for new manufacturing enterprises; guidance on financial incentives offered by Department of Commerce. Can assist with start-up capital and expansion. IDB House, 64 Chichester Street, Belfast BT1 4JX (01232 233233). Web site: www.alexandre.nics. gov.uk/idb

Local Enterprise Development Unit (LEDU)

Promotes indigenous manufacturing and service industries. Advisory service; grants and loans; government factories and sites made available. Special assistance for craftwork. LEDU House, Upper Galwally, Belfast BT8 6TB (01232 491031).

CRAFTS

Crafts Council

Promotes Britain's artist craftsmen. Offers range of schemes, including workshop training; 'new craftsmen' grants, loans and bursaries. 44a Pentonville Road, London N1 9BY (0171 278 7700).

CO-OPERATIVES

Industrial Common Ownership Movement (ICOM)

Advice and assistance with setting up worker co-operatives, especially legal structures. Consultancy, training and publications. Contact Vassalli House, 20 Central Road, Leeds LS1 6DE (0113 246 1737).

INDUSTRIAL SECTORS

British Coal Enterprise Ltd

Offers loans and business assistance to start-ups in mine-closure areas, possibly also managed workspaces. British Coal Enterprise Ltd, 232 Edwinstowe House, Edwinstowe, Mansfield, Nottinghamshire NG21 9PR (01623 826833).

British Steel (Industry) Ltd

Provides finance for growing and new businesses engaged in manufacturing or related service activities in 19 traditional steel industry areas, in England, Scotland and Wales. In some areas BS(I) also provides workspace which is primarily intended for small new businesses. British Steel (Industry) Ltd, Canterbury House, 2–6 Sydenham Road, Croydon, Surrey CR9 2LJ (0181 686 2311).

GOVERNMENT CONTACT POINTS

Government Offices for the Regions

Four departments (Employment, Trade and Industry, Environment and Transport) have been organised into integrated offices known as Government Offices (GOs) for the Regions.

Government Office for the East: Building A, Westbrook Centre, Milton Road, Cambridge CB4 1YG (01223 346700)

Government Office for the East Midlands: The Belgrave Centre, Stanley Place, Talbot Street, Nottingham NG1 5GG (0115 971 9971)

Government Office for London: 157–161 Millbank, London SW1P 4RK (0171 217 3222)

Government Office for Merseyside: Cunnard House, Pier Head, Liverpool L3 1QB (0151 224 6300)

Government Office for the North East: Wellbar House, Gallowgate, Newcastle upon Tyne NE1 4TX (0191 232 4722)

Government Office for the North West: Sunley Tower, Piccadilly Plaza, Manchester M1 4BE (0161 952 4000)

Government Office for the South East: Bridge House, 1 Walnut Tree Close, Guildford GU1 4GA (01483 882 255)

Government Office for the South West: The Pithay, Bristol BS1 2PB (0117 927 2666)

Government Office for the South West: Mast House, Shepherds Wharf, 24 Sutton Road, Plymouth PL4 0HJ (01752 221 891)

Government Office for the West Midlands: 77 Paradise Circus, Queensway, Birmingham B1 2DT (0121 212 5050)

Government Office for Yorkshire and Humberside: 25 Queen Street, Leeds LS1 2TW (0113 244 3171)

Scottish Office: Meridian Court, 5 Cadogan Street, Glasgow G2 6AT (0141 248 2855)

Welsh Office: Industry Department, Crown Building, Cathays Park, Cardiff CF1 3NQ (01222 825111)

Northern Ireland Office: Department of Economic Development, Netherleigh, Massey Avenue, Belfast BT4 2JP (01232 529900)

Local Enterprise Agencies (LEAs)

There are over 400 Local Enterprise Agencies throughout the UK, offering business advice and counselling to new and expanding businesses. Local TECs or LECs and Jobcentres can provide addresses of local LEAs. A full list of local agencies is also available from the private sector funded organisation, Business in the Community, 44 Baker Street, London W1M 1DH (0171 224 1600).

Local authorities

Many local authorities – country, district, town and borough councils – can offer help and advice to small firms. Contact the Industrial or Economic Development Officer at your local County or Town Hall. Information also usually obtainable from local library.

EXPORT

Association of British Chambers of Commerce

Export Marketing Research Scheme, 4 Westwood House, Westwood Business Park, Coventry CV4 8HS (01203 694484)

British Exporters Association

Broadway House, Tothill Street, London SW1H 9NQ (0171 222 5419)

British International Freight Association

Redfem House, Browells Lane, Feltham, Middlesex TW13 7EP (0181 844 2266)

Commission of the European Communities

Jean Monet House, 8 Storey's Gate, London SW1P 3AT (0171 973 1992)

Croner Publications Ltd

Croner House, London Road, Kingston upon Thames, Surrey KT2 6SR (0181 547 3333)

Department of Trade and Industry

Export Control Enquiry Unit, Kingsgate House, 66–74 Victoria Street, London SW1E 6SW (0171 215 5444); Web site: www.dti.gov.uk

European Commission

European Information Centres throughout the country provide an advisory service on expansion abroad and identifying partners. List of centres available from European Commission, 8 Storey's Gate, London SW1P 3AT (0171 973 1992)

Export Credits Guarantee Department (ECGD)

2 Exchange Tower, PO Box 2200, Harbour Exchange Square, London E14 9GS (0171 512 7000); Web site: www.open. gov.uk/ecqd

Institute of Export

64 Clifton Street, London EC2A 4HB (0171 247 9812)

International Chamber of Commerce

103 New Oxford Street, London WC1A 1QB (0171 240 5558)

London Chamber of Commerce and Industry

33 Queen Street, London EC4R 1AP (0171 248 4444); Web site: www.londonchamber.co.uk

NCM UK Ltd

3 Harbour Drive, Capital Waterside, Cardiff CF1 6TZ (01222 824000)

Price Waterhouse

Southwark Towers, 32 London Bridge Street, London SE1 9SY (0171 939 3000)

Simpler Trade Procedures Board (SITPRO)

Venture House, 29 Glasshouse Street, London W1R 5RG (0171 287 3525). An independent body, set up by the Department of Trade, which has developed a simplification of trade procedures and documents.

Technical Help for Exporters (THE)

British Standards Institution, 389 Chiswick High Road, London W4 4AL (0181 996 9000)

Trade Indemnity plc

12–34 Great Eastern Street, London EC2A 3AX (0171 739 4311)

Other useful addresses

The Advertising Association, Abford House, 15 Wilton Road, London SW1V 1NJ (0171 828 2771)

British Insurance and Investment Brokers Association, BIIBA House, 14 Bevis Marks, London EC3A 7NT (0171 623 9043)

British Safety Council, 70 Chancellor's Road, London W6 9RS (0181 741 1231)

British Standards Institution, 389 Chiswick High Road, London W4 4AL (0181 996 9000)

Chartered Institute of Marketing, Moor Hall, Cookham, Maidenhead, Berkshire SL6 9QH (01628 457 500)

Companies House, Crown Way, Maindy, Cardiff CF4 3UZ (01222 388588); for Scotland: 37 Castle Terrace, Edinburgh EH2 3DJ (0131 535 5800); for London: Companies Registration Office, 55 City Road, London EC1Y 1BB (0171 253 9393); Web site: www.companies-house.gov.uk

Direct Marketing Association (DMA) UK Ltd, Haymarket House, 1 Oxendon Street, London SW1Y 4EE (0171 321 2525)

Federation of Small Businesses Ltd, 32 Orchard Road, Lytham St Annes FY8 1NY (01253 720911); Web site: www.fsb.org.uk

Finance and Leasing Association, Imperial House, 15-19 Kings Way, London WC2B 6UN (0171 836 6511); Web site: www.fig-org.uk

Institute of Administrative Managers, 40 Chatsworth Parade, Petts Wood, Orpington BR5 1RW (01689 875555)

The Institute of Business Counsellors, PO Box 8, Harrogate, North Yorkshire HG2 8XB (01423 879208)

Institute of Chartered Accountants in England and Wales, PO Box 433, Chartered Accountants Hall, Moorgate Place, London EC2P 2BJ (0171 920 8100); Web site: www.icaew.co.uk

Institute of Chartered Accountants of Scotland, 27 Queen Street, Edinburgh EH2 1LA (0131 225 5673); Web site: www.cas-org.uk

Institute of Company Accountants, 40 Tyndales Road, Clifton, Bristol BS8 1PL (0117 973 8261)

The Institute of Direct Marketing, 1 Park Road, Teddington, Middlesex TW11 0AR (0181 977 5705)

Institute of Directors, 116 Pall Mall, London SW1Y 5ED (0171 839 1233)/ www.iod.co.uk

Institute of Management, Small Firms Information Service, Management House, Cottingham Road, Corby, Northants NN17 7TT (01536 204222); www/inst-mqt.org.uk

Institute of Management Consultants, 5th Floor, 32–33 Hatton Garden, London EC1N 8DL (0171 242 2140)

Institute of Personnel and Development, IPD House, 35 Camp Road, Wimbledon, London SW19 4UX (0181 971 9000)

Institute of Public Relations, The Old Trading House, 15 Northburgh Street, London EC1V 0PR (0171 253 5151)

Lawyers for Your Business, Law Society, 113 Chancery Lane, London WC2A 1PL (0171 320 5764); fyb.lawsociety.org.uk

Market Research Society, 15 Northburgh Street, London EC1V 0AH (0171 490 4911)

Marketing Society, St George's House, 3/5 Pepys Road, London SW20 8NJ (0181 879 3464)

Office of Fair Trading, Field House, 15–25 Bream's Buildings, London EC4A 1PR (0171 242 2858); www.oft.gov.uk

Patent Office. Enquiries: 25 Southampton Buildings, Chancery Lane, London WC2A 1AY (0171 438 4700). Main office: Cardiff Road, Newport, Gwent NP9 1RH (01633 814000); www.patent.gov.uk

Registrar of Trademarks, as for Patent Office above.

Royal Institution of Chartered Surveyors, 12 Great George Street, Parliament Square, London SW1P 3AD (0171 222 7000)

3i plc, 91 Waterloo Road, London SE1 8XP (0171 928 3131)

Venture Capital Report Ltd, Magdalen Centre, Oxford Science Park, Oxford OX4 4GA (01865 784411)

Premises

In addition to the 'advance factory' programme already in operation, the English Partnership (EP), in conjunction with the Department of Trade and Industry, is building small workshop premises in areas of high unemployment. Enquiries can be made direct to the EP, St George's House, Kingsway, Team Valley, Gateshead, Tyne and Wear NE11 0NA (0191 487 8941) or the Government Offices for the Regions (see pp. 205–06).

Labour relations and personnel management

Advisory, Conciliation and Arbitration Service (ACAS)

Provides a free, comprehensive advisory service on request to employers through their officers based in Scotland, Wales and several regional offices in England. Head Office: Brandon House, 180 Borough High Street, London SE1 1LW (0171 210 3000); Web site: www.acas.org.uk

Local small business clubs

These aim to further interest in small businesses by the exchange of ideas, promotion, advice and support.

NATIONAL ASSOCIATIONS REPRESENTING SMALL FIRMS

Association of British Chambers of Commerce

Co-ordinates the views of industry and commerce on matters of national and international importance and presents them to government. 9 Tufton Street, London SW1P 3QB (0171 565 2000); Web site: www.britishchambers.org.uk

Confederation of British Industry (CBI)

Represents and co-ordinates the views of small firms in its membership. Financial, economic and fiscal matters, industrial training, labour relations, technical legislation, company and commercial law. Centre Point, 103 New Oxford Street, London WC1A 1DU (0171 379 7400); Web site: www.cbi.org.uk

Federation of Small Businesses Ltd

Represents and co-ordinates the views of self-employed persons. 32 Orchard Road, Lytham St Annes, Lancs FY8 1NY (01253 720911) and at The Press and Parliamentary Office, Federation of Small Businesses Ltd, 2 Catherine Place, Westminster, London SW1E 6HF (0171 233 7900); Web site: www.fsb.org.uk

The Forum of Private Business Ltd

Represents and co-ordinates the views of small and medium-sized privately owned enterprises, including proprietors. Ruskin Chambers, Drury Lane, Knutsford, Cheshire WA16 6HA (01565 634467)

Smaller Firms Council

Centre Point, 103 New Oxford Street, London WC1A 1DU (0171 379 7400)

SOME SPECIALIST LIBRARIES

Business Statistics Office

Government Buildings, Cardiff Road, Newport, Gwent NP9 1XG (01633 815696)
An office of the Treasury. Library contains material on statistical methodology and UK official statistics – much material also available in London (Central Statistics Office). The statistical staff can occasionally assist in expanding the figures given in the various *Business Monitor* series.

Chartered Institute of Marketing Library

Moor Hall, Cookham, Maidenhead, Berkshire SL6 9QH (01628 427 500)

Department of Trade Library

Information and Library Centre, 1 Victoria Street, London SW1H 0ET (0171 215 5006/7)
Prior appointment only. Covers descriptive economics, including commercial organisations throughout the world.

Export Market Information Centre Library

Kingsgate House, 66–74 Victoria Street, London SW1E 6SW (0171 215 5444)
Comprehensive collection of UK and overseas statistics, some commercially published market surveys.

Frobisher Crescent Library at City University

Barbican, London EC2Y 8HB (0171 477 8787)
Similar to London Business School collection.

Institute of Management Library

Management House, Cottingham Road, Corby, Northants NN17 1TT (01536 204222)

London Business School Library

Sussex Place, Regents Park, London NW1 4SA (0171 262 5050)
Books and periodicals on all aspects of management, also business, economics, sociology, business law and related topics. Information files. Annual reports, press comments and some stockbrokers' reports on British and overseas companies.

London Guildhall University

School of Business Studies, 84 Moorgate, London EC2M 6SQ
(0171 320 1000)
Similar to London Business School collection.

Monopolies and Mergers Commission Library

New Court, 48 Carey Street, London WC2A 2JT (0171 324 1467)
Not open to the public but may provide information. Covers
monopolies and competition, salary surveys and industrial economics.

Office of Fair Trading Library

Field House, 15–25 Bream's Buildings, London EC4A 1PR (0171
242 2858)
Prior appointment only. Covers consumer affairs, consumer
credit, monopolies, mergers and restrictive practices.

Business Information Service

British Library – Lloyds Bank Business Line, 25 Southampton
Buildings, London WC2A 1AW (0171 412 7454/7977)
Contains those British reports on industrial markets received by
copyright deposit which are publicly available (about 10 per cent
of the total). Statistics covering particular industries or products.
Trade directories and journals.

Index

Index of
Advertisers

Getting the health and safety message across

The Health and Safety Executive (HSE) is the government body with responsibility for ensuring that risks to people's health and safety from work activities areproperly controlled. With the back-up of its inspectors and scientific specialists, HSE produces the authoritive publications on just about evert aspect of health and safety in the workplace. These publicationsn are the main and sometimes only contact HSE has with business and the public.

Your business could be breaking the law as you read this. Did you know that legally all workplaces must display the health and safety law poster or that all organisations with five or more staff must have a health andsafety policy statement?

Both of these are produced by HSE Books, the publishing arm of the Health and Safety Executive. HSE Books publish over 1500 pieces of authoritative guidance, advice and leaflets for all businesses and industries. HSE's advisory role is every bit as important as its role as enforcer of legislation, and that is why it produces such an enormous range of guidance publications.

These books won't solve all your health and safety problems but you can't build a safe workplace unless you understand basic principles like risk assessment and safeyu management. Chances are, if youre in business there is an HSE publication you could do with. HSE publishes everything from free leaflets on first aid in the workplace to priced guides to legislation and approved codes of practice. In addition HSE Books produces many titles on work with particular processes and pieces of equipment and general advice on avoiding health risks.

There is an increasing focus on small firms. While HSE has no wish to deluge them with red tape, the truth is that financial losses from accidents at work can spell disaster for many small firms. HSE Books provide the knowledge for firmsto adopt good practices, avoid the cost of accidents and run healthier and safer workplaces.

HSE priced and free publications are available from HSE Books, PO Box 1999, Sudbury, Suffolk CO10 6FS.

**Tel: 01787 881 165
Fax: 01787 313 995**